Sporting Equality

Title IX Thirty Years Later

Sporting Equality

Rita J. Simon, editor

Library of Congress Catalog Number: 2004051694
ISBN: 0-7658-0848-X
Printed in the United States of America

Library of Congress Cataloging-in-Publication Data

Sporting equality : Title IX thirty years later / Rita J. Simon, editor.
    p. cm.
    "Parts of this volume were previously published in Gender issues, spring/ summer 2002, vol. 20, nos. 2/3"—T.p. verso.
    Includes bibliographical references.
    ISBN 0-7658-0848-X (pbk.)
    1. Sports for women—United States. 2. Women athletes—Government policy—United States. 3. Sex discrimination in sports—United States. 4. United States. Education Amendments of 1972. Title IX I. Simon, Rita James.

GV709.18.U6S67 2005
796'.082—dc22

                                                        2004051694

Contents

Introduction

Sporting Equality: Title IX Thirty Years Later includes the major findings and recommendations of the Secretary of Education's Commission on Opportunities in Athletics established on June 27, 2002, as well as the Commission's Minority Report authored by Julie Foudy, captain of the U.S. Women's National Soccer Team and Donna de Varona, first president of the Women's Sports Foundation and Olympic gold medallist. Secretary of Education Rod Paige, to whom both reports were submitted, stated he would not accept the recommendations in the Minority Report and would accept only the fifteen of the twenty-three recommendations in the Majority Report that were adopted unanimously.

In addition, the collection includes articles by a member of the Commission, Lisa Keegan, chief executive officer of the Education Leaders Council, and edited versions of the testimony provided by Katherine Kersten, a senior fellow for cultural studies at the Center of the American Experiment, at the Commission's Chicago Town Hall meeting, and Andrew Zimbalist, who is the Robert A. Woods Professor of Economics at Smith College, at the Commission's San Diego Town Hall Meeting.

These pieces are followed by six chapters that analyze and assess the strength and weakness of Title IX, and offer recommendations for strengthening or changing the goals and objectives of Title IX.

Two of the chapters are by law professor Kimberly A. Yuracko, assistant professor of law, Northwestern University School of Law, "Title IX and the Problem of Gender Equality in Athletics" and Earl C. Dudley, Jr. and George Rutherglen, professors of law at the University of Virginia Law School, "A Comment on the Report of the Commission to Review Title IX Enforcement in Athletics." Barbara Murray, a graduate student in education at the University of Pennsylvania,

1

prepared a research plan on "How to Evaluate the Implementation of Title IX at Colleges and Universities and Attitudes and Interest of Students Regarding Athletics."

Professors of education John J. Cheslock and Deborah J. Anderson, both at the University of Arizona, contribute a chapter, "Lessons from Research on Title IX and Intercollegiate Athletics," that discusses how empirical research can inform the debate over Title IX given the policy environment that focuses on substantial proportionality.

The two most controversial chapters in the volume are by Leo Kocher, head wrestling coach of the University of Chicago, who claims that the manner in which Title IX has been interpreted clearly and unequivocally discriminates against male athletes, especially those in minor sports such as gymnastics, swimming, wrestling, and track; and Ellen J. Staurowsky, professor in the Department of Sport Management and Media at Ithaca College, who writes with the same stridency and sense of conviction that Title IX has not gone far enough nor has it been aggressively enforced enough to provide women athletes with the equality they deserve.

Rita J. Simon

1

Executive Summary

Secretary's Commission on Opportunities in Athletics

"Without a doubt, Title IX has opened the doors of opportunity for generations of women and girls to compete, to achieve, and to pursue their American dreams. This Administration is committed to building on those successes."—U.S. Secretary of Education Rod Paige, June 2002

On June 27, 2002, U.S. Secretary of Education Rod Paige established the Secretary's Commission on Opportunities in Athletics—the first federal advisory panel created to study Title IX. The purpose of the 15-member Commission was to collect information, analyze issues, and obtain broad public input directed at improving the application of current federal standards for measuring equal opportunity for men and women and boys and girls to participate in athletics under Title IX.

Passed by Congress as part of the Education Amendments of 1972, Title IX provides that *"[N]o person in the United States shall, on the basis of sex, be excluded from participation in, be denied the benefits of, or be subjected to discrimination under any education program or activity receiving federal financial assistance."*

As noted in the Commission's charter, prior to the enactment of Title IX many schools and post-secondary institutions were free to discriminate against women and girls. However, over the past three decades many new doors of opportunity have been opened for women and girls. In 1972, when Title IX was enacted, 44 percent of all bachelor's degrees were earned by women, as compared to 57 percent in 2000. During the same period, the percentage of women earning medical degrees increased from 9 to 43 percent. Title IX (along with changes in the view of what roles girls and women should play in society) has also had a marked impact on the athletics programs offered by educational institutions across the country. The number of women's and girl's athletic teams at both the high school and college levels has dramatically increased. From 1981 to 1999, the total number of college women's teams increased by 66 percent. The growth of certain women's sports has been explosive during this period. According to the General Accounting Office, for example, colleges created over 846 new women's soccer teams. In 1971, 294,015 girls participated in high school athletics. Today, over 2.7 million girls participate in high school athletics. This represents an 847 percent increase. It is clear, though, that more still needs to be done to ensure that girls and women are not discriminated against and that we continue to expand the array of athletic opportunities available to men, women, boys and girls. As further noted in the Commission's charter, despite the gains in athletic programs for women and girls, issues have been raised about the effectiveness of the federal government's Title IX enforcement. The questions generally fall in two areas:

- Guidance: Many college administrators claim that the U.S. Department of Education has failed to provide clear guidance on how post-secondary institutions can comply with Title IX standards and policy interpretations.
- Enforcement Activities: while many claim that the Department's Office for Civil Rights has not effectively enforced Title IX, others argue that the manner in which the Department enforces the law needlessly results in the elimination of some men's teams.

An Open and Fair Process

The Secretary charged the Commission with addressing seven key questions:

- Are Title IX standards for assessing equal opportunity in athletics working to promote opportunities for male and female athletes?
- Is there adequate Title IX guidance that enables colleges and school districts to know what is expected of them and to plan for an athletic program that effectively meets the needs and interests of their students?

- Is further guidance or other steps needed at the junior and senior high school levels, where the availability or absence of opportunities will critically affect the prospective interests and abilities of student athletes when they reach college age?
- How should activities such as cheerleading or bowling factor into the analysis of equitable opportunities?
- How do revenue producing and large-roster teams affect the provision of equal athletic opportunities? The Department has heard from some parties that whereas some men athletes will "walk-on" to intercollegiate teams—without athletic financial aid and without having been recruited—women rarely do this. Is this accurate and, if so, what are its implications for Title IX analysis?
- In what ways do opportunities in other sports venues, such as the Olympics, professional leagues, and community recreation programs, interact with the obligations of colleges and school districts to provide equal athletic opportunity? What are implications for Title IX?
- Apart from Title IX enforcement, are there other efforts to promote athletic opportunities for male and female students that the Department might support, such as public-private partnerships to support the efforts of schools and colleges in this area?

The commission addressed these seven questions in six public meetings. Beginning in July of 2002 and continuing through its last meeting in January 2003, the Commission gathered information and data representing a variety of viewpoints on Title IX and the Department of Education's enforcement standards. At four town hall meetings held in Atlanta, Chicago, Colorado Springs, and San Diego, the Commission heard from more than 50 expert witnesses representing Title IX advocacy groups, post-secondary institutions, sports governing bodies, high school and college sports associations, think tanks, and many other organizations. Each town hall meeting also offered extensive opportunities for public comment. As a result, the Commission heard directly from hundreds of parents, athletes, and administrators of elementary and secondary schools, colleges and universities. Finally, the Commission reviewed thousands of documents, reports, letters, and e-mails submitted by experts and citizens nationwide.

Recommendations

Throughout its fact-findings process, the Commission found strong and broad support for the original intent of Title IX, coupled with a great deal of debate over how the law should be enforced. The Commission also found a great deal of confusion about Title IX and a lack of clarity and guidance from the Office for Civil Rights pertaining to enforcement.

In response, the Commission adopted 23 key recommendations. Overall, the Commission found consensus on most issues. In fact, of the 23 recommendations adopted by the Commission, 15 were approved by unanimous consent. The commission wishes to draw attention to the following recommendations and the four themes that emerged with them:

Commitment

The Department of Education should reaffirm its strong commitment to equal opportunity and the elimination of discrimination for girls and boys, women and men. (Recommendation 1)

Clarity

Any clarification or policy interpretation should consider the recommendations that are approved by this Commission, and substantive adjustments to current enforcement of Title IX should be developed through the normal federal rulemaking process. (Recommendation 2)

The Department of Education's Office for Civil Rights should provide clear, consistent and understandable written guidelines for implementation of Title IX and make every effort to ensure that the guidelines are understood, through a national education effort. The Office for Civil Rights should ensure that enforcement of and education about Title IX is consistent across all regional offices. (Recommendation 3)

The Office for Civil Rights should educate educational institutions about the standards governing private funding of particular sports aimed at preventing those sports from being dropped or to allow specific teams to be added. (Recommendation 11)

Fairness

The Office for Civil Rights should not, directly or indirectly, change current policies in ways that would undermine Title IX enforcement regarding nondiscriminatory treatment in participation, support services and scholarships. (Recommendation 4)

The Office for Civil Rights should make clear that cutting teams in order to demonstrate compliance with Title IX is a disfavored practice. (Recommendation 5)

The Department of Education should encourage the NCAA to review its scholarship and other guidelines to determine if they adequately promote or hinder athletic participation opportunities. (Recommendation 13)

The Department of Education should encourage educational institutions and national athletic governance organizations to address the issue of reducing excessive expenditures in intercollegiate athletics. Possible areas to explore might include an antitrust exemption for college athletics. (Recommendation 8)

Enforcement

The Office for Civil Rights should aggressively enforce Title IX standards including implementing sanctions for institutions that do not comply. The Department of Education should also explore ways to encourage compliance with Title IX, rather than merely threatening sanctions. (Recommendation 6)

The Commission made a series of recommendations on new ways in which Title IX compliance can be measured. (Recommendations 14, 15, 17, 19, 20, 21, 23)

The Office for Civil Rights should allow institutions to conduct continuous interest surveys on a regular basis as a way of (1) demonstrating compliance with the three-part test, (2) allowing schools to accurately predict and reflect men's and women's interest in athletics over time, and (3) stimulating student interest in varsity sports. The Office should specify the criteria necessary for conducting such a survey in a way that is clear and understandable. (Recommendation 18)

Open to All: A Final Word from the Commission

The Secretary's Commission on Opportunity in Athletics is proud to offer its findings and recommendations to the Secretary. After eight months of fact-finding and deliberations, it fully understands how Title IX at thirty offers great hope to men and women athletes alike. The Commission recognizes that some of its recommendations will require additional research, including study on how Title IX relates to other important debates in post-secondary education over accountability, cost, governance, and quality. However, it is clear that Title IX enforcement requires reform in order to make the law more clear, fair, enforceable, and truly *open to all.*

2

Commission Findings

Secretary's Commission on Opportunities in Athletics

Question One: Are Title IX standards for assessing equal opportunity in athletics working to promote opportunities for male and female athletes?

Finding 1:

After 30 years of Title IX, great progress has been made, but more needs to be done to create opportunities for women and girls and to retain opportunities for boys and men.

Given the impassioned testimony presented to this Commission, there is universal consensus on one critical point: Every person who testified stated their full support for Title IX of the Education Amendments of 1972. It is uniformly agreed that this landmark law, enacted 30 years ago, has contributed greatly to opening doors of opportunity for women in our society. In announcing the Commission, Secretary of Education Rod Paige noted:

"In 1972, when Title IX became law, 44 percent of all bachelor's degrees went to women—as compared to 57 percent in 2000, the most recent year data was published. Today, the majority of college students are women. And many are entering professions that once eluded them. In 1972, only 9 percent of medical degrees went to women—as compared to nearly 43 percent in 2000. In 1972, only 1 percent of dental degrees went to women—as compared to 40 percent in 2000. And in 1972, only 7 percent of law degrees went to women—as compared to nearly 46 percent in 2000. It is no longer unusual to see women in positions of power and influence—including running large companies, ruling from the bench, or advising the President of the United States. Women fill key leadership positions throughout the Administration, including at the Department of Education. Clearly, the changes brought about with the help of Title IX have greatly expanded the opportunities for girls and women to achieve their greatest potential. And, we at the Department of Education are working to build on these successes."[32]

Title IX has also significantly influenced the opportunities afforded to girls and women to participate in athletics. Deputy Secretary of Education William D. Hansen stated in his opening remarks of the Commission's first town hall meeting in Atlanta,

"In 1971 before Title IX went into effect, more than 294,000 girls participated in high school sports. Last year that number exceeded 2.7 million, an 847 percent increase over the last 30 years. Between 1981 and 1999 the number of college women's teams rose by two-thirds. According to the General Accounting Office, our colleges created nearly 3,800 new women's sports teams, including 846 soccer teams, 516 cross country teams, 432 softball teams, 350 volleyball teams, 304 indoor track teams, and 302 basketball teams."[33]

By all accounts, Title IX has been successful in promoting athletic opportunities for women. Yet, despite this progress, the Commission heard troubling testimony that some women and girls are still subject to discrimination, both in access to athletic participation opportunities and in gaining equal treatment in facilities and support services. In some cases, there are discrepancies in the share of scholarships and budgets that cause women to lag behind men in both participation and equal treatment. It should be noted, however, that not all discrepancies in areas such as funding are a result of discrimination. Some teams may be more expensive to support than others even when the two teams have exactly the same number of participants. This is also the case with some discrepancies in financial aid, which may be caused by a disproportionate need among some athletes at a particular institution to receive academic assistance and attendance at summer school.

The Commission has also heard about unintended consequences of Title IX's application to intercollegiate athletics. The Commission heard a great deal of testimony about the troubling loss of athletic opportunities for male athletes at the collegiate level, particularly in Olympic sports such as track and field, gymnastics, and wrestling. While everyone benefits from increased athletic participation by girls and women, no one benefits from artificial limitations on athletic opportunities for either gender. Enforcement of Title IX needs to be strengthened toward the goal of ending discrimination against girls and women in athletics, and updated so that athletic opportunities for boys and men are preserved. The Commission strongly believes that Title IX has been and needs to remain an important federal civil rights statute. This philosophy was the foundation of the Commission's work, and all of our findings and recommendations were made in an effort to identify ways to strengthen Title IX.

Finding 2:

Current Title IX policy provides for three separate ways for institutions to demonstrate that they are in compliance with Title IX's participation requirement.

The policy interpretation issued by the Office for Civil Rights in 1979 created a three-part test for an institution to demonstrate compliance with the athletic participation requirement of Title IX. The three-part test provides that an institution can demonstrate that it has adequately met the athletic interests and abilities of its students if it can show that either 1) the male/female ratio of athletes is "substantially proportionate" to the male/female ratio of student enrollment, 2) the institution has a "continuing practice of program expansion" for members of the underrepresented sex, or 3) the institution is "fully and effectively" accommodating the interests and abilities of the underrepresented sex.

If properly enforced, the three-part test can be a flexible way for schools to comply with Title IX. On numerous occasions, the Commission has heard strong support for retaining the three-part test to give schools flexibility in structuring their athletics programs while guarding against freezing discrimination into place. The three-part test in theory provides flexibility for educational institutions by providing more than one way to demonstrate compliance, while also establishing attainable goals for eliminating discrimination. The Commission has heard testimony from a number of sources that many educational institutions attempt to comply solely with the proportionality part of the test while others seek to rely on parts two or three.

As will be discussed in more detail later, though, the Commission has heard numerous complaints about the three-part test. Many have argued to the Commission that because the guidance concerning the second and third parts of the test is so ambiguous, the proportionality part is the only meaningful test. Moreover many witnesses argued that the Office for Civil Rights and private litigants have transformed *substantial* proportionality into *strict* proportionality. The Commission also concluded that the test for compliance can be revitalized if the Secretary of Education will provide new guidance, while also significantly increasing efforts to reach out with educational materials.

Finding 3:

Many practitioners feel that their institutions must meet the proportionality test to ensure a "safe harbor" and avoid expensive litigation.

Witnesses and Commissioners stated on numerous occasions that attorneys and consultants have told them that the only safe way to demonstrate compliance with Title IX's participation requirement is to show that they meet the proportionality requirement of the three-part test. This part assumes that an educational institution is not discriminating in offering participation opportunities if the male/female ratio of athletes at an institution is proportional to the male/female ratio of undergraduate enrollment at that institution. It is true that many federal courts have emphasized the proportionality requirement in Title IX litigation. The facts of the *Cohen* case underscore the challenge institutions may face in meeting the evidentiary requirements of parts two and three of the three-part test, which are by their nature more subjective than part one. The court precedent reflects the decision by the Office for Civil Rights to identify only the first part of the three-part test as a "safe harbor" for demonstrating compliance with Title IX. This means that if a school can demonstrate proportionality, there will be no further scrutiny by the Office for Civil Rights. If a school claims it is in compliance under one of the other tests, the Office will scrutinize that claim more carefully since compliance under these parts is not a safe harbor. There should be an additional effort to designate parts two and three as safe harbors along with part one. For attorneys and consultants, the easily quantifiable nature of the proportionality test, requiring as it does simple data and a clear mathematical formula, may make it more likely to be favored as a means of establishing compliance. Finally, since the first part of the test is a safe harbor, if a school were to establish compliance under one of the other prongs it might still be subjected to a subsequent complaint based on its inability to demonstrate proportionality.

Finding 4:

Although, in a strict sense, the proportionality part of the three-part test does not require opportunities for boys and men be limited, it has been a factor, along with other factors, in the decision to cut or cap teams.

The 1996 clarification letter advised educational institutions that they may "choose to eliminate or cap teams as a way of complying with part one of the three-part test." Cutting teams or limiting the available places on teams is not a requirement for complying with Title IX. However, the Commission was told that when faced with a complaint regarding its athletics programs, an institution may feel that cutting a team or capping opportunities is an easy way to gain compliance.

Testimony to the Commission established that there has been an unfortunate loss of teams, particularly in non-revenue or Olympic sports. The Commission found that it is extremely difficult to obtain a set of data that is accepted by all parties. However, all agree that there has been a troubling decrease in athletic opportunities for boys and men. At the San Diego town hall meeting of the Commission, Corey Bray, director of Research in Education Services for the NCAA, noted an increase in overall participation in athletics for men and women in NCAA championship sports. However, he also noted a decrease in the average number of men's teams (–13.7%) and male athletes (–7.7%) per institution belonging to the NCAA. He noted that this information did not take into account changes in NCAA membership over time. Jerome Kravitz, a consultant to the U.S. Department of Education and professor at Howard University, also testified at the San Diego meeting and described his findings, which control for changes in NCAA membership. He found that from 1982 to 2001, women gained 2,046 to 2,384 teams and 51,967 athletic opportunities, while men lost between 1,290 to 1,434 teams and 57,100 to 57,700 participation opportunities.

The correlation between the enforcement of Title IX and this loss of teams has also been hotly contested. Many witnesses told the Commission that they believe that teams on which they participated were cut in order to comply with Title IX. The Commission believes that it is unfair to blame the loss of teams wholly on Title IX enforcement, though. Facility limitations and budgetary concerns put heavy pressure on educational institutions to cut back in their athletic programs. However, when institutions feel they must make cuts for budgetary reasons, they cannot ignore the potential effect of their decision on Title IX compliance. For instance, a school may be concerned about litigation if it cuts a women's team without being in compliance with the proportionality test.

While an educational institution could cut a team for different reasons, a GAO report indicates that there are some predominating reasons that schools give for cutting teams. These are "gender equity considerations" and facilities/budget concerns.

Finding 5:

Escalating operational costs in intercollegiate athletics threaten the effort to end discrimination in athletics and preserve athletic opportunities.

Title IX does not limit an institution's flexibility in deciding how budgets will be allocated among sports or teams. This flexibility should not be subjected to government interference, as long as those decisions are not discriminatory. There can be no question, though, that the cost of operations in intercollegiate athletics has escalated rapidly. This escalation in expenditures is often referred to as the "arms race" because as one school escalates its spending on revenue-producing sports, its competitors are required to match that move to retain competitiveness. It is clear that in some cases, this "arms race" has been the catalyst for the discontinuation of some teams. While necessary, control of the "arms race" in athletic expenditures is well beyond the province of this Commission to control. It is also clear that many, if not most, of those involved with the leadership of intercollegiate athletics already recognize the need for national action related to the escalation. This Commission, though, would like to state its sense that all avenues must be explored in order to allow institutions to realize potentially great savings by reining in the "arms race." This savings could be the means of retaining some opportunities that might otherwise be lost.

It should be noted in this discussion that the Commission is mindful of the fact that the majority of educational institutions are Division II and III schools where the "arms race" considerations do not necessarily apply. While these institutions are faced with budgetary constraints, the issues are quite different than those that face Division I programs that are funded in part through revenue-producing sports. It should be noted that many of the athletic opportunities that have been lost have occurred at the Division II and III levels.

Question Two: Is there adequate Title IX guidance that enables colleges and school districts to know what is expected of them and to plan for an athletic program that effectively meets the needs and interests of their students?

Finding 1:

There is great confusion about Title IX requirements caused by a lack of clarity in guidance from the Office for Civil Rights.

Discussion among Commissioners and testimony offered to the Commission has indicated a widespread sense that the Office for Civil Rights has not provided enough clarity to help institutions to understand how they can establish compliance with Title IX. The confusion has involved each portion of the three-part test, but particularly the second and third parts. This confusion may result from a number of factors. Among these might be: 1) misunderstanding or ignorance about the exact nature of the requirements for Title IX compliance, 2) a lack of education by the Office for Civil Rights on the nature of the three-part test, 3) a lack of clarity in the second and third parts of the test, and 4) a need for additional technical assistance and practical examples of the ways in which institutions can comply. Some have suggested that the Equity in Athletics Disclosure Act contributes to confusion about Title IX compliance by focusing only on the relative rates of participation that would be used for the first part of the test. This might give the impression that this first part is the only effective part of the test.

With regard to the first part of the three-part test, some administrators and others felt they had received conflicting information about the nature of the "safe harbor" concept and the meaning of strict proportionality. As described above, the first part of the three-part test has been designated by the Office for Civil Rights as a "safe harbor" for demonstrating compliance with Title IX's participation requirement. Some have suggested that this gives institutions the sense that only by complying with the first part of the test can they avoid a finding of discrimination in their athletic programs. Thus, schools may feel pressure to achieve proportionality as quickly as possible regardless of how it is accomplished.

With regard to the second part of the test, there has been confusion expressed about how an institution can determine whether it is in compliance. Specifically, clarity is needed regarding the phrase "continuous expansion," and in the requirement that an educational institution must create a new women's team to comply with this test. Some have pointed to schools with an early and rapid expansion of opportunities for women but which have not made changes recently, as potentially being penalized by a requirement that teams be added continually. Similarly, some athletics directors believe their predecessors put off the appropriate expansion of opportunities for women and thus left the new director dangerously out of compliance. There has also been much testimony questioning the fairness of allowing a school to ignore the other parts of the three-part test by intermittently adding programs for women.

With regard to the third part of the test, some administrators express confusion about the possibility of using interest surveys to periodically determine levels of student interest in athletics, which then must be met with matching levels of athletic opportunity. In addition, schools expressed some concern about whether they must approve every request for recognition of a new women's team regardless of financial limitations to accommodate student interest. Thus, some witnesses have argued that if an educational institution is involved with litigation for dropping or failing to add a women's team, that fact alone would preclude a finding that they had accommodated student interest.

This wide range of confusion about the three-part test indicates a need for further information from the Office for Civil Rights about the precise meaning of these tests and the available means for complying with them. Indeed, some schools may be making decisions that may limit the athletic opportunities of their students because those schools do not understand what Title IX actually requires of them.

It is also extremely important to note that any confusion institutions feel about Title IX guidance is greatly exacerbated when schools receive contradictory guidance on compliance from different regions of the Office for Civil Rights. Because administrators may seek information on compliance from their peers in other institutions, differing standards in the regional offices of the Office for Civil Rights can have wide repercussions. Consistency across regions should be a high priority in the effort to clarify the requirements of the three-part test.

A final concern is that absent a strong, clear voice from the Office for Civil Rights about the exact nature of Title IX's requirements, an abundance of information from sources about how to comply with Title IX (such as from attorneys, private consultants, the NCAA, campus organizations and other national groups) may only add to the confusion. Administrators need to understand the legal requirements of Title IX clearly so they can evaluate advice from these other sources.

Finding 2:

The Office for Civil Rights' enforcement of Title IX can be strengthened.

Complaints to the Commission about enforcement of Title IX by the Office for Civil Rights have focused on a few areas. First, some have complained that the process of enforcement is not sufficiently transparent and that sharing of settlement letters might add transparency to the process. Second, concern has been expressed that the enforcement of Title IX is not sufficiently strong since federal funding has never been withheld from a school for failure to comply. Obviously, the hesitancy to use this penalty might be explained by the enormous effects it would have on a school's educational mission. However, some have suggested that the Office for Civil Rights may have other available sanctions short of this with which to encourage compliance.

Question Three: Is further guidance or other steps needed at the junior and senior high school levels, where the availability or absence of opportunities will critically affect the prospective interests and abilities of student athletes when they reach college age?

Finding 1:

Currently, in structuring their athletic programs, colleges are not appropriately responsive to athletic participation at the high school level.

Although there has been some discussion about issues related to Title IX compliance at the high school level, the small amount of such testimony and the expertise of the Commissioners does not allow for extensive findings on how high schools are complying with Title IX.

One important theme that has emerged has been the identification of a disconnect between high school and college athletic programs in terms of the respective opportunities they make available. While high school athletic participation for boys and girls has been steadily increasing, the nature of college athletics makes it possible for only a relatively small number of high school athletes to be able to participate in varsity sports at the college level. Thus, cuts in specific programs for men and women at the college level may severely limit the opportunities for boys and girls who participate in those sports in high school. The Commission heard testimony indicating that colleges are not always sensitive to national and regional trends in student interest at the high school level.

The Commission heard arguments that Title IX enforcement may contribute to this situation by encouraging schools to add certain teams or drop others solely to increase the relative participation percentages for students of one sex. While this may help to create the impression of opportunity, it does not necessarily best serve the interests of the high school students who will eventually be served by the college system.

In response to this disconnect, it has been suggested that if colleges are careful to factor in demonstrated athletic interest at the high school level, there may be a greater likelihood that a larger number of student athletes will be able to participate in college athletics.

Question Four: How should activities such as cheerleading or bowling factor into the analysis of equitable opportunities?

Finding 1:

The Office for Civil Rights utilizes flexible guidelines in helping schools determine whether an activity is a sport.

In response to a request from Commissioners, the Commission's staff requested information from a number of national groups and the Office for Civil Rights regarding how they define a sport. The aim of the questions was to gauge whether Title IX enforcement appropriately allows institutions to assess their compliance with the participation requirements of the Title IX regulations given emerging athletic opportunities that may not have traditionally been considered sports (so-called "emerging sports"). Commission staff sent a series of questions to six organizations: the NCAA, NAIA, NFHS, NJCAA, and the Office for Civil Rights.

The results, which were presented to all of the Commissioners, indicated that most national organizations define sports through a vote of their members. The NCAA and NFHS have more detailed criteria for determining what is a sport. However, the NCAA definition of "emerging sports" is limited to women's athletic opportunities. In contrast, the Office for Civil Rights does not have a definition of sports used in assessing the participation opportunities available at individual institutions. Instead, it offers technical assistance to educational institutions to help them identify whether or not activities they sponsor are athletic opportunities for purposes of Title IX compliance. This approach allows for flexibility for schools in determining which sports they will offer for their students.

The five factors identified by the Office for Civil Rights for determining whether a particular activity is a "sport" are: 1) whether the selection of teams/participants is based on factors related primarily to athletic ability; 2) whether the activity is limited to a defined season; 3) whether the teams/participants prepare for and engage in competition in the same or similar way as other teams/participants in the interscholastic or intercollegiate athletics program (e.g., with respect to coaching, recruitment, budget, try-outs and eligibility, and length and number of practice sessions and competitive opportunities); 4) whether the activity is administered by the athletic department; and 5) whether the primary purpose of the activity is athletic competition and not the support or promotion of other athletes. These criteria allow institutions wide latitude in counting participation in emerging sports as athletic opportunities for purposes of Title IX compliance. In addition, some of the national organizations reporting to the Commission have indicated an expansion in the types of activities they recognize as sports opportunities for students. The NCAA, for instance, recognizes nine sports as emerging sports for women, including bowling and squash. Similarly, the NAIA recognizes women's wrestling as an emerging sport. The NFHS lists 13 emerging sports and state athletic associations may include even more. For instance, the Michigan High School Athletic Association recognizes competitive cheerleading as a sport and recently added a state championship in bowling.

Thus, emerging sports, including cheerleading and bowling as well as many others, may help schools meet their commitment to offer athletic participation opportunities to their students that meet the requirements of Title IX if they meet the guidelines of the Office for Civil Rights.

One concern expressed by some Commissioners, though, is that the Office for Civil Rights criteria are not necessarily widely disseminated to school administrators. This may prevent them from benefiting from the flexibility provided by the guidelines.

Question Five: How do revenue producing and large-roster teams affect the provision of equal athletic opportunities? The Department has heard from some parties that whereas some men athletes will "walk-on" to intercollegiate teams—without athletic financial aid and without having been recruited—women rarely do this. Is this accurate and, if so, what are its implications for Title IX analysis?

Finding 1:

Title IX does not require mirror image men's and women's sports programs.

Current Title IX enforcement standards consider the total participation opportunities afforded each gender by an institution's athletics program, rather than the numbers or sizes of teams sponsored by the school. So, when the Office for Civil Rights examines whether an athletic program complies with Title IX's participation requirement, it does not look at the relative similarity of teams offered to either sex, but at the ways in which the school accommodates the interests and abilities of athletes. This means that Title IX does not impose a requirement that each women's team be matched by a corresponding men's team or vice versa. This appropriately allows institutions to structure their programs to reflect the relative interests on that specific campus. This allows for nondiscriminatory reasons to be factored into an institutional decision to offer opportunities that might otherwise appear inequitable (such as a team with equipment expenses or roster sizes higher than another team).

As has been noted before, Title IX does not require a school to offer any athletic opportunities if it so chooses. But when a school makes a choice to do so, it must ensure that there is no discrimination in its decision of which opportunities to make available. Outside of the requirement of nondiscrimination, the Office for Civil Rights assumes that schools will wisely tailor the programs they offer to the interests and abilities of the student body at that institution.

Finding 2:

Artificial limits on walk-on opportunities do not benefit anyone.

Although no statistical analysis of this issue has been performed, there has been much testimony about the relative rates at which men and women walk-on to teams. A walk-on athlete is one who participates in a sport without either full or partial scholarship support for their participation. A number of witnesses have told Commissioners that male athletes currently walk-on to teams at greater levels than do females. It has been alleged that this has led institutions to limit the number of men allowed to walk-on to teams, a practice known as roster management. Roster management may control the appearance of disproportional participation, but it does not create any corresponding benefit for the sex not subject to roster management.

The relative differences in rates at which men and women walk-on to teams has been explained by reference to cultural forces encouraging male sports participation, which are not matched by a corresponding set of forces for women. It has also been suggested that since women are more involved in a number of other extracurricular activities, they may be simply exercising their choices in ways different to those of men. There is wide consensus, though, that even if the interest of men and women in taking advantage of walk-on opportunities is not the same, no one should be discouraged from walking on to teams for artificial reasons.

Artificial reasons may include: 1) cutting down on the number of opportunities available to one sex in order to ensure compliance with the proportionality part of the three-part test, and 2) avoiding the creation of new opportunities for women by limiting the number of men who can participate. A situation where one sex loses the opportunity to walk-on to teams where no corresponding benefit to the other sex is gained is not the intent of Title IX enforcement. Limiting walk-ons for reasons other than those related to lack of institutional resources or coaching decisions has serious ramifications for students who are not allowed to participate in athletics. Schools should not impose these kinds of artificial barriers to such participation.

Finding 3:

Since Congress has previously declined to exempt revenue-producing sports from Title IX consideration, any change in that policy would have to be generated by Congressional action.

While the Commission has not heard much support for exempting revenue-generating sports from Title IX consideration, some such attempts have been made in the past. On a number of occasions, Congress considered and either rejected or failed to act on proposals to exempt football, men's basketball and other revenue-producing sports from Title IX compliance. The first was the failed Tower Amendment to the Title IX statute. The question of differential treatment for revenue-producing sports arises because some witnesses claim that schools favor revenue-producing sports to the exclusion of other sports. Others respond that the revenue generated by some teams is used to support other athletic opportunities provided by the school.

Question Six: In what ways do opportunities in other sports venues, such as the Olympics, professional leagues, and community recreation programs, interact with the obligations of colleges and school districts to provide equal athletic opportunity? What are the implications for Title IX?

Finding 1:

Opportunity at the Olympic and professional levels enhances student interest in participating in these sports in high school and collegiate programs.

In its work, the Commission has concentrated on the myriad issues surrounding Title IX enforcement. There is, however, an important role for other sports venues to play in issues related to Title IX. The Commission recognizes the great benefit athletic participation has for boys and girls. Testimony before the Commission established that not all participation at the earliest ages takes place in a school setting. Community leagues and private sports clubs may involve many more students than elementary and secondary schools in certain sports, such as gymnastics. In addition, high profile professional and Olympic contests increase student interest in athletics. Nowhere is this more obvious than in the surge in popularity of soccer following the victory of the U.S. Women's Soccer Team in the 1996 Olympics. Although these kinds of opportunities do not change the legal requirements for compliance with Title IX, they fuel the interest that makes Title IX viable. They ought, therefore, to be encouraged.

Question Seven: Apart from Title IX enforcement, are there other efforts to promote athletic opportunities for male and female students that the Department might support, such as public-private partnerships to support the efforts of schools and colleges in this area?

Finding 1:

An increase in allowable scholarships for women's sports might help schools to come into compliance with Title IX.

The Commission heard limited discussions about the role of nonpublic entities in fostering athletic interests and opportunities. One very specific matter that received the attention of the Commission is the role of the NCAA's scholarship limits on creating opportunities in athletics. It has been suggested that increasing the allowable scholarships for some women's sports might help schools effectively attract more female athletes and thus better comply with Title IX. That might also allow schools to balance out the disparities caused when large numbers of men walk-on to teams without having scholarships. It would allow schools that have complained about not being able to fill their rosters on some women's teams to seek out women who would participate with the effective incentive of financial assistance.

COMMISSION RECOMMENDATIONS

Based on its findings, the Commission provides the following recommendations to the Secretary of Education. The Commission urges the Secretary to give these recommendations serious consideration and study. The recommendations are in italics with a brief explanatory paragraph following. Recommendations unanimously approved by the Commission are noted with an asterisk.

Recommendation 1*:

The Department of Education should reaffirm its strong commitment to equal opportunity and the elimination of discrimination for girls and boys, women and men.

A clear consensus emerged that affirmed Title IX's importance as a major federal civil rights statute that has brought about tremendous advancements in our society. The Commission heard no testimony recommending that Title IX be repealed or even revised. The Commission recognizes that while women and girls have had many new opportunities, there is much more that must be done. Title IX will continue to be a critical component of our nation's quest for fairness.

Recommendation 2:

Any clarification or policy interpretation should consider the recommendations that are approved by this Commission, and substantive adjustments to current enforcement of Title IX should be developed through the normal federal rulemaking process.

The Commission heard criticism that the current interpretation of Title IX was implemented through non-regulatory processes. The Commission strongly recommends that any new Title IX policies or procedures be subject to public notice and comment, and that the Administrative Procedures Act be strictly adhered to. When the public is given an opportunity to comment on proposed rules, the new rules can be improved by those comments. Moreover, the new rules are given legitimacy when this process is followed.

Recommendation 3*:

The Department of Education's Office for Civil Rights should provide clear, consistent and understandable written guidelines for implementation of Title IX and make every effort to ensure that the guidelines are understood, through a national education effort. The Office for Civil Rights should ensure that enforcement of and education about Title IX is consistent across all regional offices.

This recommendation addresses the widespread confusion expressed about the specific requirements of Title IX compliance and the importance of making the guidance on Title IX from the Office for Civil Rights clear, understandable, and arrived at in a transparent way. As noted in the findings, the Commission has heard complaints about inconsistency in advice on Title IX compliance across regional offices of the Office for Civil Rights. This recommendation aims to prevent this, and the confusion it causes, for educational institutions conscientiously trying to comply with the law.

Recommendation 4*:

The Office for Civil Rights should not, directly or indirectly, change current policies in ways that would undermine Title IX enforcement regarding nondiscriminatory treatment in participation, support services and scholarships.

Given the widespread support for and success of Title IX, the Department of Education should not change policies in a way that would threaten any progress in creating athletic opportunities for women. It should also be understood that the Commission in no way seeks to lessen the importance of institutional requirements related to nondiscrimination in facilities and support services although these are not discussed at length in this report.

Recommendation 5*:

The Office for Civil Rights should make clear that cutting teams in order to demonstrate compliance with Title IX is a disfavored practice.

The loss of teams described in the Commission's findings, and eloquently described by many of the people affected, have caused the Commission great concern. Although the Commission recognizes that the decision to drop a team is affected by many factors, it should be made clear to schools that it is not a favored way of complying with Title IX. The fundamental premise of Title IX is that decisions to limit opportunities should not be made on the basis of gender. Therefore, educational institutions should pursue all other alternatives before cutting or capping any team when Title IX compliance is a factor in that decision. If indeed teams have to be cut, student athletes should be given justification and adequate notice.

Recommendation 6*:

The Office for Civil Rights should aggressively enforce Title IX standards, including implementing sanctions for institutions that do not comply. The Department of Education should also explore ways to encourage compliance with Title IX rather than merely threatening sanctions.

Testimony before the Commission has noted that no school has been denied federal funding for failure to comply with Title IX. Although this is a dramatic enforcement mechanism, it is still available when there is no compliance. Other mechanisms should be pursued with educational institutions that encourage compliance and are not necessarily punitive.

Recommendation 7*:

The Department of Education should encourage educational and sports leaders to promote male and female student interest in athletics at the elementary and secondary levels to encourage participation in physical education and explore ways of encouraging women to walk on to teams.

In addition to enforcement of Title IX, much should be done to encourage interest in athletics. The Commission recommends that the Department of Education explore innovative programs to support and nurture a strong interest in athletics and physical fitness. The Commission recommends that the Department explore this issue closely with the President's Council on Physical Fitness. The Department should also consult with national sports organizations, foundations, and professional sports leagues about increasing their commitment to developing youth sports programs. The Commission believes that if young girls and boys are participating in large numbers in youth sports programs, our culture will continue to change so that athletic opportunities at the intercollegiate level will come to include equal opportunities for women.

Recommendation 8:

The Department of Education should encourage educational institutions and national athletic governance organizations to address the issue of reducing excessive expenditures in intercollegiate athletics. Possible areas to explore might include an antitrust exemption for college athletics.

One of the major factors identified by the Commission in the decision to cut teams is the lack of resources at some schools. The Commission has also heard much testimony about ever-mounting expenditures on college athletics that may exacerbate the problem. Sound use of financial resources will contribute to the continuation of broad sports programs that include Olympic sports. The Commission believes that the Department of Education could make helpful suggestions related to this matter. One Commissioner expressed opposition to an antitrust exemption for college athletics.

Recommendation 9*:

The Department of Education should encourage the redesign of the Equity in Athletics Disclosure Act so that it provides the public with a relevant and simplified tool to evaluate the status of Title IX compliance in the nation's post-secondary institutions.

The Commission has heard that the current form for Equity in Athletics Disclosure Act reporting may contribute to the sense that schools need to comply solely with the first part of the three-part test. The Commission also felt that the form should be significantly simplified. Since this form was created legislatively, any change would come about through Congress, so this recommendation is framed as a suggestion of encouragement the Department of Education can give to Congress.

Recommendation 10*:

The Office for Civil Rights should disseminate information on the criteria it uses to help schools determine whether activities they offer qualify as athletic opportunities.

In its work, the Commission sensed a lack of understanding of the guidelines developed by the Office for Civil Rights to help schools determine whether activities they support are sports opportunities for purposes of Title IX compliance. This recommendation would remedy that.

Recommendation 11:

The Office for Civil Rights should educate educational institutions about the standards governing private funding of particular sports aimed at preventing those sports from being dropped or to allow specific teams to be added.

Some witnesses testified that their teams might not have been cut if their schools had been allowed to receive outside funding to support the team. This recommendation would encourage the Office for Civil Rights to disseminate information on current standards for schools considering acceptance of outside funding of sports programs.

The members of the Commission who opposed this recommendation felt that, although they did not endorse exempting private funding of specific teams, the Office for Civil Rights should be allowed to find ways in which to ensure outside funds to teams could be accepted.

Recommendation 12:

The Office for Civil Rights should reexamine its regulations regarding the standards governing private funding of particular sports aimed at preventing those sports from being dropped or to allow specific teams to be added.

This recommendation reflects the same concerns as that of the previous one. It encourages the Office for Civil Rights to review the standards by which outside individuals or groups may make contributions to sports programs at educational institutions. The Commissioners noted in regard to this recommendation that total exemption of sport-specific funding would not be appropriate under this recommendation.

In distinction, some Commissioners were concerned that the current regulations are adequate and need not be revisited. They opposed this recommendation because they felt that revisiting current rules might open the door to discriminatory funding practices where teams would receive large donations that would only benefit one sex. One Commissioner felt this would be analogous to a race-specific scholarship donation.

Recommendation 13*:

The Department of Education should encourage the NCAA to review its scholarship and other guidelines to determine if they adequately promote or hinder athletic participation opportunities.

The last finding of the Commission noted that changes in scholarship limits by the NCAA might provide opportunities for schools to promote opportunities in athletics. This recommendation is aimed at the NCAA, which determines allowable scholarships.

Recommendation 14*:

If substantial proportionality is retained as a way of complying with Title IX, the Office for Civil Rights should clarify the meaning of substantial proportionality to allow for a reasonable variance in the relative ratio of athletic participation of men and women while adhering to the nondiscriminatory tenets of Title IX.

The Commission has been told that the meaning of the term "substantial proportionality" in the first part of the three-part test has been adjusted in practice to require "strict proportionality." This recommendation would clarify the meaning of "substantial proportionality."

Recommendation 15:

The Office for Civil Rights should consider a different way of measuring participation opportunities for purposes of allowing an institution to demonstrate that it has complied with the first part of the three-part test. An institution could establish that it has complied with the first part of the test by showing that the available slots for men and women as demonstrated by the predetermined number of participants for each team offered by the institution, is proportional to the male/female ratio in enrollment.

This option would allow a school to demonstrate that it has made athletic opportunities available. Even if the slots a program makes available are not filled, the school could still be in compliance with the first part of the three-part test. It would also remove artificial limitations on the walk-on athletes at an institution.

Some Commissioners who opposed this recommendation argued that since walk-on athletes receive institutional resources they should be treated the same as other athletes. In response to the concern with capping men's opportunities, they said that teams may be capped for reasons unrelated to Title IX. Finally, they stated that this recommendation did not take into consideration the possibility that female enrollment may be lower due to disparities in recruiting men and women to educational institutions.

Recommendation 16*:

In providing technical assistance, the Office for Civil Rights should advise schools, as necessary, that walk-on opportunities are not limited for schools that can demonstrate compliance with the second or third parts of the three-part test.

Since the second and third parts of the three-part test do not take into consideration the relative male/female athletic participation rates, educational institutions that want to allow large numbers of walk-on athletes should be encouraged to consider reaching compliance through parts two and three of the three-part test.

The concerns expressed by some Commissioners about the previous recommendation were also voiced in response to this one.

Recommendation 17:

For the purpose of calculating proportionality with the male/female ratio of enrollment in both scholarships and participation, these ratios will exclude walk-on athletes as defined by the NCAA. Proportionality ratios will be calculated through a comparison of full or partial scholarship recipients and recruited walk-ons.

As described in the findings, the Commission feels that artificial limitations on the number of walk-ons may limit opportunities without any corresponding gain for the underrepresented sex. This recommendation aims at removing those artificial limitations.

Some commissioners expressed a concern with this recommendation because they believe that differential treatment for walk-on athletes would not be appropriate since these athletes receive resources from their institutions as do other athletes.

Recommendation 18:

The Office for Civil Rights should allow institutions to conduct continuous interest surveys on a regular basis as a way of (1) demonstrating compliance with the three-part test, (2) allowing schools to accurately predict and reflect men's and women's interest in athletics over time, and (3) stimulating student interest in varsity sports. The Office should specify the criteria necessary for conducting such a survey in a way that is clear and understandable.

Some schools have complained that they have no quantifiable way of demonstrating compliance with the third part of the three-part test. This recommendation directs the Department of Education to develop specific guidance on interest surveys and how these surveys could establish compliance with the three-part test.

Those Commissioners opposed to this recommendation believe that allowing interest surveys may prevent future progress in providing opportunities for women because offering opportunities regardless of interest may encourage participation even where none currently exists. They felt that any use of interest surveys should be limited to demonstrating compliance with the third part of the three-part test. They also faulted the recommendation for not taking into consideration the effect of historical patterns of discrimination on women's interest in athletics.

Recommendation 19*:

The Office for Civil Rights should study the possibility of allowing institutions to demonstrate that they are in compliance with the third part of the three-part test by comparing the ratio of male/female athletic participation at the institution with the demonstrated interests and abilities shown by regional, state or national youth or high school participation rates or national governing bodies, or by the interest levels indicated in surveys of prospective or enrolled students at that institution.

This recommendation provides another way for schools to quantify compliance with the three-part test.

Recommendation 20:

In demonstrating compliance with the proportionality requirement of the first part of the three-part test, the male/female ratio of athletic participation should be measured against the male/female ratio of an institution's undergraduate population minus nontraditional students.

The Commission has heard testimony indicating that nontraditional students are much less likely to participate in athletics than other students. This recommendation recognizes that phenomenon and is aimed at allowing colleges to comply with Title IX where it would be difficult to do so based on large numbers of students who, based on their circumstances, are extremely unlikely to participate in varsity sports.

The Commissioners opposing this recommendation believe that non-traditional students may be as interested in sports as any other students and should thus not be excluded from consideration in determining proportionality under the first part of the three-part test. They also argued that part three of the three-part test already allows for variances caused by nontraditional students at an educational institution.

Recommendation 21*:

The designation of one part of the three-part test as a "safe harbor" should be abandoned in favor of a way of demonstrating compliance with Title IX's participation requirement that treats each part of the test equally. In addition, the evaluation of compliance should include looking at all three parts of the test, in aggregate or in balance, as well as individually.

Many who have testified before the Commission have complained that the emphasis of the Office for Civil Rights on encouraging compliance with the first part of the three-part test by designating it as a safe harbor is leading institutions to limit opportunities rather than expand them. This recommendation aims to allow schools to demonstrate compliance using the other parts of the test without having to be concerned about later complaints for noncompliance with the first part.

Recommendation 22*:

The Office for Civil Rights should be urged to consider reshaping the second part of the three-part test, including by designating a point at which a school can no longer establish compliance through this part.

The Commission has heard testimony that the second part of the three-part test may no longer be necessary because schools have had since 1972 to comply with Title IX and there is no longer a need to allow them to phase-in compliance. It has also heard that the second part is so unclear as to make it almost impossible to use to demonstrate compliance with Title IX. This recommendation urges the Office for Civil Rights to examine the continued viability of the second part of the test and ways of making it more understandable.

Recommendation 23*:

Additional ways of demonstrating equity beyond the existing three-part test should be explored by the Department of Education.
Over the years, changes in the demographics of athletic participation and college enrollment have made Title IX enforcement more complicated. As these kinds of changes continue, there may be further need to allow educational institutions to comply with Title IX requirements beyond those currently in place.

Recommendations Which the Commission Neither Approves nor Disapproves (Defeated by a Tie Vote):

Institutions governed by Title IX standards, as one approach to meeting the standard of proportionality, should allot 50 percent of their participation opportunities for men and 50 percent for women. A variance of 2 to 3 percent in compliance with this standard would then be allowed.
This recommendation would dramatically alter the current enforcement of Title IX in order to provide more quantifiable goals for compliance while still providing some flexibility to allow for uncontrollable changes in athletic programs such as dropouts, loss of eligibility, and walk-ons.

3

Minority Views on the Report of the Commission on Opportunity in Athletics

Donna de Varona and Julie Foudy

EXECUTIVE SUMMARY

We are today releasing a Minority Report to fully set forth our views on the issues posed by the Secretary of Education to the Commission on Opportunity in Athletics. We are compelled to issue this Report because we were not allowed to include within the Commission's own report a full discussion of the issues and our position on the recommendations that have been adopted. Our concerns are the following:

- The findings and recommendations of the Commission's report fail to address key issues or to reflect an understanding of the discrimination women and girls still face in obtaining equal opportunity in athletics.
- Many of the recommendations approved by the Commission would seriously weaken Title IX's protections and substantially reduce the opportunities to which women and girls are entitled under current law.
- The omissions and weaknesses of the Commission's report are the result of a process that did not adequately focus on critical issues, did not compile evidence necessary to address the state of gender equity in our nation's schools, and did not allow sufficient time for Commissioners to review the record or provide sufficient information for them to assess the impact of their recommendations.

The Commission's Report Fails to Include
Crucial Findings and Recommendations

Our Minority Report sets forth numerous findings that are not included—or are discussed only cursorily and without a full presentation of the evidence or the issue—in the Commission Report. Among them are the following:

- The Title IX athletics policies have been central in the effort to expand opportunities for women and girls and eliminate discrimination against them. The policies have been in place through Republican and Democratic Administrations, and have been upheld by every one of the eight federal appellate courts that has reviewed them.
- Discrimination against women and girls still exists, and the current athletics policies are still necessary to continue to make progress toward equal opportunity.
- Women are not less interested in playing sports than men. This unlawful stereotype is contradicted by the facts, which show huge increases in women's participation since Title IX was passed. Women's lower level of participation reflects persistent discrimination against them, not lack of interest.
- Advances for women and girls have not resulted in an overall decrease in opportunities for men.
- In the cases where men's teams have been cut, budgetary decisions and the athletics arms race are the true culprits.

The recommendations set forth in our Minority Report flow from these critical findings. In brief, we recommend that the Department of Education:

- Protect the current Title IX athletics policies without change—they are fair, flexible and have opened doors for millions of young women and girls in sports.
- Enforce Title IX to eliminate the continuing discrimination against women and girls in athletics.
- Educate schools and the public about the flexible way Title IX actually works, that there are three different ways to comply, and that cutting men's teams is disfavored.
- Encourage schools and athletic organizations to rein in escalating athletics costs and agree on reforms so that more female and male athletes will have a chance to play.

- Review whether some rules, like athletic association scholarship limits, make it more difficult for schools to comply with Title IX.
- Require high schools to report data on the gender breakdown of sports teams and expenditures.

The Commission's Recommendations Would Seriously Weaken Title IX and Substantially Reduce Opportunities for Women and Girls to Play Sports

We believe that the Commission's key recommendations would seriously weaken Title IX standards and authorize schools to take steps that would further disadvantage women and girls on the playing field. *As our report shows, these recommendations could result, in one year alone, in the loss of tens of thousands of participation opportunities, and millions of dollars in scholarships, from those to which women and girls are entitled under current law.* They would also undermine fundamental civil rights principles by enshrining the stereotype that women are less interested in playing sports than men.

Among the problematic recommendations:

- Recommendations 15, 17 and 20 would undercut Prong One of Title IX's three-part test and substantially reduce the number of athletic opportunities to which women and girls are entitled by permitting schools to count male and female students and athletes in new ways. These recommendations would:
  — Allow schools to count an open-ended number of "ghost slots" for athletes. This would enable schools to artificially inflate the percentage of athletic opportunities they give to women by counting opportunities they never actually fill or seek to fill. This is particularly problematic since women, on average, receive only 32% of athletic recruiting budgets.
  — Allow schools to exclude all unrecruited walk-ons from their count of athletes, no matter how large the number, even though these players get the benefits of sports participation. This recommendation would enable schools to pretend that they are not giving athletics opportunities to men, and then to reduce their obligation to female athletes accordingly. *In one school alone, excluding nonscholarship athletes from the count would result in 86 fewer slots for women—a reduction of 26% from the opportunities to which they are entitled under current law.*
  — Exclude so-called "non-traditional" students—including students over

the age of 24 and students of any age who are parents—from the count of students, which would seriously hurt women. Under this proposal, schools would be authorized to assume, for purposes of Title IX, that no older student or student with children is interested in playing sports. This stereotype is both inaccurate and contrary to basic civil rights law.

- The Unnumbered Recommendation and Recommendation 14 would treat schools as having provided equal opportunity even where they do not actually provide it, by allowing "variances" from equal opportunity standards. This means that schools could be deemed to be in compliance with Title IX participation requirements without providing proportionate opportunities or satisfying any other prong of the three-prong test. *Annual losses of 50,000 opportunities and $122 million in scholarships for collegiate athletes, and 305,000 opportunities for female high school athletes—or more—could result from these recommendations alone.*

- Recommendations 18 and 19 would authorize improper use of interest surveys to limit opportunities for girls and women and to weaken Prong Three of the three-part test. These recommendations would allow schools to conduct interest surveys of the type rejected by courts—interest surveys that have been found to measure the persistence of discrimination against women and girls, not the interest that exists when girls are given unfettered participation opportunities. The recommendations would force women and girls to prove their right to equal opportunity before they are given a chance to play, something the courts have said is inconsistent with Title IX. *For example, Brown University tried unsuccessfully to use the principles behind these recommendations to allow it to drop two entire women's teams.*

- Recommendation 12 would authorize the Secretary of Education to create a loophole in discrimination law by allowing private donors to underwrite men's teams without triggering any obligation that women's teams be treated equally.

- Recommendation 23 offers the Secretary an open-ended invitation to add new ways to comply with Title IX that were not even considered by the Commission. This recommendation could authorize other radical changes to Title IX policies that would weaken protections for women and girls.

These Recommendations Result from a Flawed Process

The recommendations are the result of a process that prevented full consideration of the relevant issues. In particular:

- The Commission's charge failed to ask the critical question: whether discrimination against girls and women persists, and how it can be remedied.
- The Commission lacked representatives of important constituencies, including Division II and Division III colleges and high school athletes.
- Witnesses selected by the Department of Education testified two-to-one against current policies, and other expert testimony that was requested was not provided.
- The Commission had inadequate time for serious review of the record or the report.
- The Commission was not provided information on, nor therefore was able to consider, the impact of its recommendations.
- The arrangements made for expression of minority views were insufficient. Because the Commission authorized only short statements of minority views, but did not allow for any fuller statement of the dissenters' rationales, the report does not reflect a full statement of the views of each Commissioner.

Conclusion

Equal opportunity for women and girls in education is of the utmost importance to our nation. Although women and girls have made great strides toward equality in the 30 years since Title IX was passed, there is much more to be done before Title IX's goals are achieved. As a result, we urge the Secretary to reject Recommendations 12, 14, 15, 17, 18, 19, 20, 23 and the Unnumbered Recommendation and to keep current policies in place without change. Rather than changing these long-standing and vital policies, the Department should focus on using the policies to educate schools and the public about the importance and flexibility of the law. The goal of equal opportunity cannot be the subject of negotiation; Title IX's vision, and the important policies that serve it, must be preserved. Americans deserve no less.

REPORT

In June 2002, Secretary of Education Roderick Paige created the Commission on Opportunity in Athletics to evaluate whether and how current standards governing Title IX's application to athletics should be revised. The Commission is today transmitting its report to the

Secretary, a report that includes recommendations for substantial changes to current Title IX guidelines and policies.

After careful review and deliberation and unsuccessful efforts to include adequate discussion of our minority views within the majority report, we have reached the conclusion that we cannot join the report of the Commission. We are instead releasing this Minority Report and request that the Secretary include this document in the official records of the Commission's proceedings.

Our decision is based on (1) our fundamental disagreement with the tenor, structure and significant portions of the content of the Commission's report, which fails to present a full and fair consideration of the issues or a clear statement of the discrimination women and girls still face in obtaining equal opportunity in athletics; (2) our belief that many of the recommendations made by the majority would seriously weaken Title IX's protections and substantially reduce the opportunities to which women and girls are entitled under current law; and (3) our belief that only one of the proposals would address the budgetary causes underlying the discontinuation of some men's teams, and that others would not restore opportunities that have been lost.

This Minority Report is divided into three sections. The first presents the findings and recommendations that we believe the Commission should have included in its report—a substitute report. The second section addresses the reasons that we cannot support a number of the Commission's key recommendations. The third section identifies some of the problems with the Commission's process that we believe contributed to the problems with the report and with the recommendations that will weaken Title IX's protections.

With regard to this last point, in our view, the problems with the report are the result of a process, established by the Commission staff, that did not adequately focus on critical issues, did not compile all of the evidence necessary to fully address the state of gender equity in our nation's schools, and did not allow sufficient time for Commissioners to conduct either a careful review of the evidence that *was* compiled or an assessment of the potential impact of various recommendations.

We ask that the Commissioners and Secretary give careful consideration to this Minority Report. Title IX has been one of our country's most important and most effective civil rights laws, and the public deserves the fullest possible education about, access to, and consideration of, the issues at stake in the important debate about the law's application to athletics. Ensuring that Title IX's goal of equal opportunity is reached demands no less.

PART I: FINDINGS AND RECOMMENDATIONS

A. Findings

Finding 1

Title IX, and the three-part test, have promoted great advances for women and girls to participate in sports.

Title IX, and the three-part test that implements it, have opened doors for millions of women and girls to obtain the benefits of participating in competitive athletics. While fewer than 32,000 women participated in college sports prior to the enactment of Title IX,[1] today that number has expanded nearly five-fold—or more than 400%—to approximately 163,000 women.[2] Opportunities for girls at the high school level have grown even more dramatically; since 1972, female participation in high school athletics has skyrocketed by 847%, from 294,000 to almost 2.8 million.[3]

Finding 2

Despite these advances, discrimination still limits athletics opportunities for girls and women at both the high school and college levels today.

Despite Title IX's success in opening doors to women and girls, the playing field is far from level for them. For example, although women in Division I colleges are 53% of the student body, they receive only 41% of the opportunities to play sports, 36% of overall athletic operating budgets, and 32% of the dollars spent to recruit new athletes.[4] Girls at the high school level receive 1.1 million fewer opportunities to play sports than their male counterparts.

Among other things, these disparities affect women's access to the financial assistance that can increase the ability to pursue a college education; it has been estimated that men receive $133 million more *per year* than women in athletic scholarships.[5] Additionally, women at all educational levels continue to be subjected to inequities in the treatment of their teams, from inferior equipment and facilities to disadvantageous scheduling and opportunities to receive coaching.

Table 1
Net Outcome of Added and Discontinued Teams

	1981–82	1998–99	Change in Number of Teams	Percentage Change
Female	5,695	9,479	+3,784	66%
Male	9,113	9,149	+36	.4%

Source: GAO Report—*Four-Year Colleges' Experiences Adding and Discontinuing Teams, 2001*

Finding 3

Enhancing athletic opportunities for young women and girls is of vital importance because of the significant benefits those opportunities provide.

Competitive athletics promotes physical and psychological health; responsible social behaviors; greater academic success; and increased personal skills.[6] A recent study by the Oppenheimer Fund found that more than four out of five executive businesswomen (82%) played sports growing up—and the vast majority say lessons learned on the playing field have contributed to their success in business.[7] And for low-income women and girls, the financial support made available through athletics scholarships can mean the difference in being able to attend college at all.

Finding 4

The fact that women and girls have fewer opportunities in athletics than men reflects the persistent discrimination against them, not lack of interest.

Although the Commission heard allegations that women are less interested in participating in sports than men, the history of Title IX flatly contradicts this assertion. The dramatic increases in participation at both the high school and college levels since Title IX was passed show that when doors are opened to them, women and girls will rush through. And the fact that 2.8 million girls play sports in high school refutes any claim that there is insufficient interest to fill the approximately 170,000 slots now available to participate in intercollegiate athletics or the additional opportunities to which they are entitled under the law.

Courts have repeatedly recognized that the stereotype that women are less interested in sports than men is unfounded and unlawful. As one court stated, "interest and ability rarely develop in a vacuum; they evolve as a function of opportunity and experience. [W]omen's lower rate of participation in athletics reflects women's historical lack of opportunities to participate in sports."[8]

Finding 5

Advances in opportunities for girls and women have not resulted in an overall decrease in opportunities for men.

The Commission heard testimony that there has been an unfortunate loss of men's teams, particularly in non-revenue and Olympic sports. Yet, while men on some teams have lost opportunities, those losses have been offset by increases in the number of men playing other sports. Men's intercollegiate athletic participation rose from approximately 220,000 in 1981–82 to approximately 232,000 in 1998–99. Between 1981–82 and 1998–99, football participation increased by 7,199, more than offsetting wrestling's loss of 2,648 participants, outdoor track's loss of 1,706 participants, tennis's loss of 1,405 participants, and gymnastics' loss of 1,022 participants. Other sports that gained participants include baseball (+5,452), lacrosse (+2,000), and soccer (+1,932).[9] In addition, as Table 1 makes clear, the number of men's teams increased over this same time period.

Finding 6

When Title IX was weakened in the past, men's teams, particularly wrestling, did not benefit.

Between 1984 and 1988, when a Supreme Court decision suspended application of Title IX to intercollegiate athletics programs and the three-part test was not in effect, colleges and universities cut wrestling teams at a rate almost three times as high as the rate of decline in the 12 years following, when Title IX's application to athletics was reestablished. In the four-year period between 1984 and 1988, the number of NCAA institutions sponsoring men's wrestling teams dropped by 53, from 342 to 289—or approximately 13.3 teams per year. Between

1988 and 2000, that number dropped by 55, from 289 to 234—or approximately 4.6 teams per year.[10]

Finding 7

The three-part test, adopted by the Department of Education in 1979 and in force since that time, is flexible and fair. All three prongs of the test have been used successfully by schools to comply with Title IX and each is necessary to give schools flexibility in structuring their athletics program while guarding against freezing discrimination into place.

The three-part test offers three wholly independent ways that schools can show that they are providing equal opportunities to their male and female students to participate in athletics. Schools can show that:

- The percentages of male and female athletes are substantially proportionate to the percentages of male and female students; or
- The school has a history and continuing practice of expanding opportunities for the underrepresented gender; or
- Even if it is not providing proportionate opportunities, the school is fully and effectively meeting its female students' interest and ability to participate in sports.

Each of the prongs offers a viable means to comply with Title IX's participation requirements, and each has been successfully used by schools. Indeed, the General Accounting Office has found that between 1994 and 1998, more than two-thirds of the schools investigated by the Office for Civil Rights and the Department of Education complied with Title IX's participation requirements under prong two or prong three.[11]

The three-part test as a whole provides substantial flexibility. The first part of the test stands for the basic principle that a school that provides equal opportunity to the women and the men in its student body is, by definition, not discriminating against any of those students. It does not mandate proportionality; it simply authorizes a school to treat women equally with men and says the law will approve it when they do. It is this common-sense principle that has led courts to call this prong of the test a "safe harbor." But if members of one gender are underrepresented among an institution's athletes, this does not mean that the school has not complied with Title IX; it simply means that the school could use one of the other two prongs to demonstrate that it meets Title IX requirements.

The second prong allows schools to show that they have made, and are continuing to make, progress toward equality. And the third prong permits schools to customize equal opportunity requirements to their own campuses, by providing a lower level of opportunity to women where that lower level nonetheless satisfies the interests and abilities that exist. It is difficult to conceive of an enforcement mechanism that could more flexibly accommodate the myriad types of athletic programs that exist on our nation's campuses, as well as the differences among student bodies at different schools, and still be true to the core principles of Title IX's mandate of equality.

Finding 8

The Office for Civil Rights (OCR) has provided extensive guidance on the operation of each prong of the three-part test, but should provide enhanced technical assistance, consistent with that guidance, on the means by which schools can comply with the test. OCR can also do more to ensure consistent interpretation of Title IX by all regional offices.

When it was adopted in 1979, the three-part test was part of a larger Policy Interpretation that described in detail the OCR approach to assessing compliance with Title IX in the area of athletics. In January 1996, the OCR issued a Clarification of the 1979 Policy Interpretation. This Clarification provides specific factors to guide an analysis of each prong, as well as multiple examples to demonstrate, in concrete terms, how each of these factors is applied. Among other issues, the Clarification addresses in detail: (a) how to define an "athlete" for purposes of evaluating proportionality; (b) circumstances in which schools will be given leeway, and need not provide precisely proportional opportunities, under prong one of the test; (c) factors that OCR will consider in assessing whether a school has a history and continuing practice of expanding opportunities; (d) the means by which schools should assess the interests of their students under prong three; and (e) the means by which schools should assess whether there is sufficient ability and expectation of competition to sustain a team under that prong. The numerous examples included throughout the Clarification offer a valuable roadmap for schools seeking to understand the operation of each prong of the test.

The Commission heard testimony that there is confusion about the terms of the three-part test and about the flexibility provided by current Department policies. More technical assistance about the means by which schools can comply with the test, as well as about best practices—as identified, for example, in the 2001 GAO Report—might help to address any confusion that exists. In addition, OCR should ensure that any complaints about inconsistent enforcement by different OCR regional offices are addressed.

Finding 9

The term "safe harbor," used by some courts and OCR to describe the operation of the first prong of the three-part test, is a legal term of art that does not mean that the first prong is the only effective way to comply with the test. OCR can do more to provide enhanced technical assistance to ensure that educational institutions understand that compliance is possible under Prongs One, Two or Three.

In its 1996 Clarification, OCR—using language from the court's decision in *Cohen v. Brown University*—described the first prong of the three-part test as a "safe harbor" for schools. By that designation, OCR used a well-known legal term that, in this context, means simply that schools that can meet the terms of the first prong can evaluate their compliance with no additional inquiry. The term "safe harbor" is a protection for the institution, but does not mean that the first prong is the only "safe" way to comply with Title IX's participation requirements or that it is more difficult to meet the standards of prongs two and three of the test. The term is a merely descriptive one that adds no legal weight to the operation of the first prong.

Finding 10

The lawfulness of the three-part test has been affirmed by every federal appellate court to consider the issue.

The three-part test has been the subject of substantial litigation since its adoption, in cases brought both by women who assert that they have been denied participation opportunities and by men who claim that the three-part test has resulted in cuts to their teams. In *every* case that has been brought, the federal court of appeals hearing the case has upheld the three-part test and the policies then in place to implement it. Eight out of eight circuit courts have considered the issue and found that the test appropriately implements Title IX requirements.[12] It is well-settled law, and to change it would unleash a new round of litigation, causing real confusion and uncertainty.

Finding 11

OCR has never imposed a financial penalty on a school for failing to comply with the three-part test.

Although permitted to do so by Title IX, OCR has never imposed on a school the penalty authorized for a failure to comply with Title IX: the loss of federal funding.

Finding 12

The three-part test does not impose quotas or require preferential treatment.

Because athletic teams are sex-segregated, schools *themselves* decide how many slots they will allocate to men and how many to women. The proportionality prong does not dictate how many slots, that would otherwise be open to all, must be set aside for women—it merely offers a means of measuring whether the school is dividing the sex-segregated slots it has created on an equal basis. As every appellate court to address the issue has recognized, "determining whether discrimination exists in [sex-segregated] athletic programs *requires* gender-conscious, group-wide comparisons."[13]

Finding 13

Title IX does not require mirror image men's and women's sports programs.

Current Title IX enforcement standards consider the total participation opportunities afforded each gender by an institution's athletics program, rather than the numbers or sizes of teams sponsored by the schools. Title IX does not impose a requirement that each women's team be matched by a corresponding men's team or vice versa. Similarly, Title IX does not require that men and women be granted equal numbers of athletic scholarships, but only that overall scholarship dollars be allocated equitably among male and female athletes.

Finding 14

Title IX does not cause cuts to men's teams.

Nothing in Title IX or its policies requires schools to reduce men's opportunities to come into compliance with participation requirements. In fact, GAO data confirm that 72% of colleges and universities that have added women's teams have done so without cutting any teams for men.[14] Additionally, although the Commission was provided with less information on this issue, women's teams have also suffered cuts over the last 20 years. For example, the number of schools sponsoring women's gymnastics dropped from 190 in 1981–82 to 90 in 1998–99—a decline of more than 50%.[15]

Finding 15

To the extent that schools have discontinued men's—and women's—athletic teams since Title IX was passed, there are many reasons for those decisions. Most notably, budgetary decisions, the athletics "arms race," excessive expenditures, and philosophical decisions related to the appropriate quality and size of athletic programs have resulted in the loss of opportunities for other sports.

Title IX does not limit an institution's flexibility in deciding how budgets will be allocated among sports or teams. There can be no question, though, that the cost of operations in intercollegiate athletics has escalated rapidly. This escalation in expenditures is often referred to as the"arms race" because as one school escalates its spending on revenue-producing sports, its competitors feel required to match that move to retain competitiveness. It is clear from testimony that this "arms race" has been the catalyst for the discontinuation of many teams. And the Commission received substantial information on the spiraling costs of coaching salaries, perquisites for players, and luxurious athletic facilities that increasingly strap college athletics budgets and force reductions in other expenditures for sports.

Finding 16

Rules set by the National Collegiate Athletic Association (NCAA) could be hampering schools' ability to comply with Title IX.

The Commission heard testimony that the NCAA limits the number of scholarships that colleges and universities can provide to their male and female athletes. While they do not dictate the level of participation opportunities, these scholarship limits could nonetheless be hampering schools' efforts to provide equal opportunities for women. If, for example, a school could demonstrate that it had the financial resources to expand the scholarship benefits for a current women's team but not to create a new team, it would merit further inquiry to determine if NCAA limits hinder that approach. The same is true for other NCAA rules that may have problematic consequences.

Finding 17

"Walk-on" student-athletes cost money and receive the benefits of participation in intercollegiate athletics. To the extent that men walk on more than women, intangible benefits accorded to men's teams and the persistent budgetary barriers that limit the extent to which women's teams can support additional players have been identified as causes.

Walk-on athletes—typically, those players who do not receive athletic scholarships—receive the benefits that stem from participation in athletics, including coaching, practice, training services, medical benefits, equipment, uniforms, preferential course scheduling, academic support programs, pre-season training period room and board, access to weight rooms, and the like. It is clear that provision of these services to additional athletes costs money. In addition, the addition of walk-on athletes to a team forces a school to reconsider its coaching ratios to ensure that all players receive adequate attention. As a result, there are costs and competitive considerations that influence a school's decision whether to limit the permissible number of walk-ons.

Women's teams often lack the resources to provide for more than the minimum number of athletes slated by the school for the team. Additionally, because of the history of discrimination to which female athletes have been subject, women's teams sometimes lack the status of their men's counterparts. To the extent that men walk on to teams to a greater degree than women, these factors have been identified as causes.

Finding 18

The Office for Civil Rights uses flexible guidelines in helping schools determine whether an activity is a sport.

The Office for Civil Rights has identified five factors that schools can use to determine whether particular activities are sports for purposes of evaluating compliance with Title IX's participation requirements. These criteria preserve school flexibility and should be widely circulated as part of OCR's technical assistance activities.

Finding 19

There is a mechanism by which the Department of Education can systematically monitor participation in athletics and athletic program expenditures at the college levels—the Equity in Athletics Disclosure Act. There is no mechanism in place by which the Department of Education or the public can systematically monitor these variables at the high school level.

The Equity in Athletics Disclosure Act requires colleges and universities to compile data about the gender breakdown of their participation opportunities and scholarship dollars, as well as about their expenditures on, and recruiting and coaching expenses for, men's and women's teams. Because the EADA does not apply to secondary schools, there is no comparable requirement that high schools monitor how they are allocating sports opportunities between their male and female students.

B. Recommendations

Recommendation I

The Department of Education's current Title IX athletics policies, which have promoted advances toward equality for women in sports, should be preserved without change.

The Department's current athletics policies, in place through Republican and Democratic administrations and upheld by every federal appellate court to examine them, have worked to open doors to millions of girls and women to gain the benefits of participating in competitive sports. The playing field is not yet level, however, and the policies must be maintained in order to ensure that women and girls receive the truly equal opportunity they are afforded by the law.

Recommendation 2

The Department of Education should strongly enforce Title IX standards, including implementing sanctions for institutions that do not comply.

Enforcement should be strengthened, and resources increased, to ensure that discrimination is investigated and addressed in an effective and timely way.

Recommendation 3

Using existing guidance, Department of Education staff should undertake an educational campaign to help educational institutions understand the flexibility of the law, explain that each prong of the three-part test is a viable and independent means of compliance, and give practical examples of the ways in which schools can comply.

Although there is ample guidance, as described in the Findings, that sets forth the standards of current law, some witnesses expressed confusion about the terms of existing policies. The Department should consider assigning resources to enable schools to consult with Department personnel and secure technical assistance during the process of structuring their athletics programs. The Department should also ensure that copies of its guidance are widely distributed to all Department civil rights personnel, at headquarters and in the field, and to educational institutions at all levels of education. It would also be helpful were OCR to place all intercollegiate and interscholastic athletics closure letters and corrective action agreements on its website. Posting of such materials would allow athletics directors and school administrators to identify acceptable solutions and time frames for correcting participation problems.

Recommendation 4

In educating schools about current policies, the Department of Education should advise them that nothing in Title IX requires the cutting or reduction of men's teams, and that to do so is disfavored.

Numerous civil rights laws apply the principle of "equalizing up" in authorizing remedies for discrimination—that is, raising opportunities for the disadvantaged group, rather than diminishing them for the previously benefited group, as a means of achieving civil rights compliance. In providing technical assistance, the Department should advise schools of this principle, as well as providing information on techniques other schools have used to achieve this goal.

Recommendation 5

The Department of Education should encourage educational institutions and national athletic governance organizations to address the issue of reducing the escalating costs of intercollegiate athletics, particularly in some parts of the men's athletics programs, and fostering agreement on reforms.

The Department of Education should play a critical role in establishing and facilitating forums in which these issues can be addressed, as well as in publicizing and seeking agreement to their results. The reduction of excessive athletics expenditures would go a long way toward freeing up resources to support both women's teams and men's lower profile sports. The Department should also initiate conversations about more systemic reforms to eliminate the "arms race" in athletics—reforms that would allow reallocation of resources to support broad-based sports participation by both male and female students.

Recommendation 6

The Department of Education should encourage educational institutions and national athletic governance organizations to address whether organization rules, such as limitations on the numbers of athletics scholarships, hamper compliance with Title IX participation requirements and, if so, to take corrective action.

Because certain rules, including those of the NCAA, may have turned out to hinder colleges and universities from taking feasible steps to comply with Title IX participation requirements, this issue is ripe for study. As with issues related to controlling escalating costs, the Department could and should play a valuable role in convening and fostering dialogue to address these issues and remedy any problems that are found.

Recommendation 7

The Department of Education should require secondary schools to compile and report the data currently required of colleges and universities under the Equity in Athletics Disclosure Act.

Collection of these data would provide the Department and the public with a valuable tool to assess the status of gender equity in high schools and to monitor school attempts to come into compliance with Title IX requirements. Legislation has recently been introduced by Senator Snowe (R-ME), and the Department should consider supporting that bill. The Department in any event has the administrative authority to require collection of this data even absent legislative action.

PART II: RESPONSES TO COMMISSION RECOMMENDATIONS

The Commission's Majority Report asserts that the recommendations made by the Commission are the product of "strong consensus." However, we strongly disagree with the Commission's major recommendations, and, for a number of them, were joined by other Commissioners as well. We believe that these recommendations are contrary to the intent of Title IX, would critically weaken this important civil rights law, and would result in substantial losses of participation opportunities and scholarships for women. We summarize our concerns below.

A. Three Recommendations Would Substantially Reduce the Number of Athletic Opportunities to which Women and Girls are Entitled by Permitting Schools to Count Male and Female Students and Athletes in New Ways.

A number of the Commission's recommendations authorize schools to change the ways in which they count the men and women in their student bodies, on the one hand, and the men and women to whom they provide athletic opportunities, on the other. Singly and together, these recommendations would allow schools to be deemed as complying with Title IX while substantially reducing the number of participation opportunities they are obliged to provide to women under current standards.

Recommendation 15 would modify the proportionality prong of the three-part test by allowing each school to identify a "predetermined number of participants for each team offered by the institution" and then to count that number of slots as filled—regardless of how many athletes in fact participate on the team. This proposal would allow schools to artificially inflate the percentage of athletic opportunities they give to women by counting opportunities they never actually fill or seek to fill.

The potential for abuse that is inherent in this proposal has long been recognized. In fact, the Office for Civil Rights rejected just such a recommendation in issuing the 1996 Policy Clarification. In determining the number of participation opportunities offered by a school, OCR refused to count "unfilled slots, i.e., those positions on a team that an institution claims the team can support but which are not filled by actual athletes," because "participation opportunities must be real, not illusory" and because "OCR must consider actual benefits provided to real students."[16] To allow a school to count slots which provide *no* actual benefits to *any* real student would make a mockery of any claim that the school was providing equal opportunity.

The recommendation is all the more problematic because women lag significantly behind men in the receipt of dollars spent to recruit new athletes. The average Division I college allocates only 32% of its athletic recruiting budget to women's teams.[17] It is particularly troubling for a school that spends 112% more recruiting men than women—and that then, as a result, has fewer women participating on its women's teams—to be able to claim credit for providing a "predetermined," but unfilled, number of slots. If Title IX's participation requirements are interpreted in a way that provides no check on these disparities, women will continue to be treated as second-class citizens in schools' recruiting efforts.

Recommendation 17 would also allow schools to change the ways in which they count the athletic opportunities they provide, by allowing schools *not* to count athletic opportunities for men that the schools actually *do* provide. Recommendation 17 provides that proportionality ratios should be "calculated through a comparison of full or partial scholarship recipients and recruited walk-ons," excluding from the count opportunities provided to walk-on athletes as defined by the NCAA.

This proposal would enable schools to pretend that they are *not* giving athletics opportunities to men, and then to reduce their obligation to female athletes accordingly, even though walk-on athletes receive the benefits of sports participation, including coaching, training, tutoring, equipment and uniforms. In fact, by one estimate, a school that excluded from its count athletes who did not receive scholarships could reduce its participation gap and thereby reduce by 32 the number of slots to which women would be entitled under current law.[18] This decline in the participation gap is a wholly illusory and artificial reduction; it does not signify that the school has in fact made any progress whatsoever in providing equal opportunities to its male and female students.

Further, it is unclear, as a practical matter, how this recommendation would apply to Division III colleges or to high schools, where athletes are provided no scholarships. Under Recommendation 17, therefore, only "recruited walk-ons" would count in the school's totals. But unlike Division I and II schools, Division III colleges are not required by the NCAA to monitor contacts between coaches and prospective students; as a result, they do not have the means to evaluate whether their walk-on athletes are "recruited" under the NCAA definition. Moreover, Division III schools often lack the funding to send coaches on recruiting trips or to phone or bring prospective athletes to campus. Consequently, large numbers of athletes are likely *not* to have been recruited under NCAA standards, even though they may have been recruited in other ways. Because this proposal does not address whether Division III schools could claim that their athletes are *not* recruited, or what standards regarding recruitment would apply, there could be an even larger loophole in Title IX's protections at Division III colleges—even beyond the impact of the proposal on Division I and Division II schools.

Recommendation 20 provides that in demonstrating compliance with the proportionality prong of the three-part test, "the male/female ratio of athletic participation should be measured against the male/female ratio of an institution's undergraduate population minus nontraditional students." Under this proposal, in other words, schools could exclude so-called "non-traditional" students—defined for this purpose to include students who are not between the ages of 18 and 24[19] and students of any age who have children—as members of the student body whose interests and abilities the schools are obligated to accommodate.

The stereotype that students over a certain age or students who are parents are not interested in participating in sports is both inaccurate and contrary to many Supreme Court cases that have struck down these types of stereotypes. This recommendation would allow every school to presume, for purposes of Title IX, that all students who are over the age of 24 or who have children are uninterested in playing sports. That is unfair to women, who are disproportionately likely to be the "non-traditional" older students excluded under this proposal. Available data show, for example, that among individuals older than 24 who were enrolled in degree-granting institutions in 2001, women outnumbered men by 37%. [20] It is also impractical; in order to equitably apply the principle of exclusion based on parental status, the school would have to identify and exclude not only mothers, but also male undergraduates, of any age, who have fathered children.

The recommendation is also unnecessary, because schools that enroll large numbers of "non-traditional" students are, like other schools, specifically authorized under prong three of the test to consider the interests of that population in allocating their athletic opportunities. To the extent that a school's female students, including those who are "non-traditional," are in fact less interested in participating in sports than men, the school will be in compliance with Title IX if it fully accommodates the interest that exists—even if it falls short of proportionality.

B. Two Recommendations Would Treat Schools as Having Provided Equal Opportunity Even Where They Do Not Actually Provide It.

Two of the recommendations would authorize schools to comply with a proportionality standard without actually providing equal opportunity to their female students—and without satisfying any other prong of the three-part test.

An unnumbered proposal, which is included in the report although it received only a tie vote, would direct schools to allocate 50% of their participation opportunities to men and 50% to women regardless of the actual percentage of males and females in the student body, and then authorize schools to fall short of that allocation by 2–3 percent-

Table 2
Lost Opportunities and Scholarships under Unnumbered Recommendation,
Which Could Be Even Greater under Recommendation 14

	50/50 Standard with +/- 2% Variance (Females = 48%)	*50/50* Standard with +/- 3% Variance (Females = 47%)
Collegiate Female Athletes	43,000	50,000
Scholarship Losses for Collegiate Female Athletes	$103,000,000	$122,000,000
Participation Losses for High School Female Athletes	163,000	305,000

age points. This proposal would, in effect, allow schools to impose a ceiling of 47% of athletic opportunities and scholarships for women— no matter how large the percentage of women in the student body or how many women want to play. Because women typically comprise 53% of the student body at Division I-A schools, and 49% of the students at the high school level, this proposal will inevitably result in losses from the opportunities to which women and girls would be entitled under current law. The losses are, of course, likely to be greater at the numerous colleges at which women comprise a higher percentage than 53% of undergraduates—including some powerhouse institutions, such as Florida State University and the University of Georgia, where women are 57% of the student body. Table 2 illustrates the projected annual losses at each educational level, assuming no reduction in current participation or scholarship opportunities for men, college enrollment of 53% female (average enrollment at Division I-A schools), and high school enrollment of 49.1% female (national average enrollment in grades 9–12).

Similarly, Recommendation 14 urges the Secretary to allow for a "reasonable variance" from equality if proportionality is retained as a way of complying with Title IX. Because the language is open-ended, it is impossible to put a limit on the losses that girls and women would endure were this recommendation to be adopted; in fact, this proposal could result in greater losses than those anticipated under the unnumbered proposal. This recommendation would authorize the Secretary to treat as sufficient for Title IX compliance a level of participation that falls far short of true equality—subject only to his own, subjective judgment about what is a "reasonable" variance. While we did not object to this recommendation when it was proposed following a confused and truncated Commission discussion, our review of it as drafted in the Commission's report convinces us that it could create damaging results that would not be consistent with Title IX and that we cannot support.

C. Two Recommendations Would Authorize Improper Use of "Interest Surveys" to Limit Opportunities for Girls and Women and to Weaken Prong Three of the Three-Part Test.

Recommendation 18 would allow schools to use "interest surveys" to (a) demonstrate compliance with the three-part test; (b) "accurately predict and reflect men's and women's interest in athletics over time"; and (c) stimulate student interest in sports. Because it would authorize the use of such surveys to reduce schools' obligations to provide equal opportunity to women and girls, this recommendation is fundamentally flawed in numerous respects.

First, the use of interest surveys to reduce the basic obligation of educational institutions to provide equal opportunity is invalid and has been unequivocally rejected by the courts. Using interest surveys is a way to force girls and women to *prove* their right to equal opportunity before giving them a chance to play. The proposal rests on the stereotyped notion that women are inherently less interested in sports than men—a notion that contradicts Title IX and fundamental principles of civil rights law.

As courts have repeatedly recognized, what interest surveys measure is the discrimination that has limited opportunities for girls and women to participate in sports—*not* the interest that exists when girls are given unfettered opportunities to play. As the court in *Cohen v. Brown University* put it, "interest and ability rarely develop in a vacuum; they evolve as a function of opportunity and experience.... [W]omen's lower rate of participation in athletics reflects women's historical lack of opportunities to participate in sports."[21] To allow the use of surveys to limit opportunities for women is simply to freeze prior discrimination into place—it certainly is not to "accurately predict and reflect men's and women's interest in athletics over time."

Additionally, the evidence proves that women are *not* less interested in sports than men; when the doors of opportunity are opened, women rush through them. As noted above, girls' and women's participation in sports has increased dramatically since the passage of Title IX 30 years ago. Moreover, it is simply illogical to claim that women are less interested in obtaining the economic, physical, psychological and social benefits that stem from participation in athletics. There are 2.8 million girls participating in high school sports, and fewer than 170,000 opportunities to play in college; this fact is alone sufficient to demonstrate that the argument that women are not interested in sports is simply an effort to continue an outmoded stereotype.

Recommendation 19, as described in the Commission's report, suffers from some of the same flaws as Recommendation 18. Recommendation 19 advises the Secretary to study allowing schools to assess compliance with the third prong of the three-part test by comparing the school's ratio of male/female athletic participation to the "demonstrated interests and abilities" shown by high school and other participation rates or by interest levels shown in surveys of current or prospective students at the school. To the extent that this recommendation was intended or would be used to authorize restriction of opportunities for girls and women based on the results of an interest survey—or to modify the third prong of the test to allow merely "relative" rather than full accommodation of the women's interests and abilities that exist—it directly contradicts the court's ruling in *Cohen v. Brown University*. In its 1996 Clarification, OCR has set forth explicit and detailed guidance on the appropriate and lawful ways to evaluate interest and abilities under the third prong of the test, and that guidance must be maintained intact. Upon review of the report's treatment of this recommendation, we cannot agree to it unless the understanding set forth above is made clear.

D. One Recommendation Would Allow Schools to Use Private Funding to Subvert Equal Opportunity for Girls and Women.

Recommendation 12 requests the Office for Civil Rights to reexamine its policies governing the private funding of teams to prevent sports from being dropped or to allow specific teams to be added. Current law is more than adequate to allow such private funding; what supporters of this recommendation apparently have in mind is to enable the Secretary to rewrite long-standing policy to permit private donors to underwrite men's teams without triggering any obligation that schools then treat their women's teams equally. Were the Secretary to accept this invitation, schools could also be authorized to steer private slush funds to male teams without counting them as athletes—or, in other words, to create a loophole that would justify discrimination if subsidized by private funds.

We support having the Office for Civil Rights provide technical assistance to educate schools and the public about the existing standards governing private funding of teams—but only to the extent that Title IX principles and limitations are respected and conveyed in the process.

E. One Recommendation Offers the Secretary an Open-Ended Invitation to Add New Ways to Comply with Title IX Not Even Considered by the Commission.

Recommendation 23 advocates that the Secretary explore "additional ways of demonstrating equity beyond the existing three-part test." This open-ended proposal could be used to authorize changes to Title IX enforcement mechanisms that the Commission never even addressed, much less approved. Given that the three-part test has stood the test of time—and has been affirmed by both Republican and Democratic administrations and uniformly upheld in the courts—it is inappropriate, particularly when substantial discrimination still exists to be remedied, for the Commission to be proposing what could amount to a wholesale abandonment of this critical enforcement tool. Our careful review of this recommendation in the report—and our analysis of the threat it represents to current policies, which we were unable to conduct under the time constraints of the Commission meeting—convince us that we must withdraw our original consent to this proposal.

There are other recommendations whose meaning, upon review of the Commission's written report, seems ambiguous. Recommendation 9, for example, encourages redesign of the Equity in Athletics Disclosure Act to provide the public with a "relevant and simplified tool" to evaluate a school's Title IX compliance. While it would be unobjectionable to change EADA reporting requirements to allow schools to supply additional information about their compliance with the three-part test, it would be contrary to our intent in consenting to this recommendation, and contrary to the purpose of the reporting obligation, to use this recommendation to justify an overhaul of the reporting form that would delete key information. We would strongly disagree with any interpretation of this or any other recommendation that would lead to a reduction of the protections in place for girls and women to achieve equal opportunities to participate in athletics.

PART III: PROBLEMS IN THE COMMISSION'S PROCESS

We have set forth above some of the concerns that trouble us about the recommendations that the Commission has now approved. We believe that the problems with the recommendations reflect problems in the Commission process that prevented full consideration of the relevant issues:

- **The Commission's charge failed to ask the critical question: whether discrimination against girls and women persists, and how it can be remedied.** The Commission's charter did not contain the question that should have informed the Commission's efforts from the beginning. Instead, the Commission's focus was on addressing losses to some men's teams. As a result, the Commission made no inquiry into the question whether the original goals of Title IX have been met—and if not, why.
- **The Commission lacked representatives of important constituencies.** There was no Commissioner who represented the interests and perspectives of Division II or Division III schools, or junior and community colleges. Most significantly, the Commission lacked any representative of high school athletics programs. The Commission's report itself acknowledges the Commission's inability to reach conclusions about the application of Title IX at the high school level; this is a particularly troubling omission because the recommendations, if adopted by the Secretary, will affect the nearly 6 million students who play sports in high school.
- **Witnesses selected by the Department of Education testified two-to-one against current policies, and other expert testimony that was requested was not provided.** The witnesses who were invited to testify were overwhelmingly opposed to current Title IX policies, while witness testimony from supporters of the law was limited. For example, the Department of Education invited at least five panelists from schools sued for failure to comply with Title IX, but selected no witnesses to represent plaintiffs who were victims of discrimination or women whose teams had been cut.

Moreover, Commissioners requested specific experts whose testimony would have helped inform critical components of the Commission's inquiry. The Department of Education declined to invite these requested experts. To choose just two examples, the Commission did not hear from the author of the authoritative GAO report on participation trends, who would have testified that men's participation opportunities and number of teams have increased, not decreased, over time. In addition, the only witness who was asked to testify about current law was a recent law graduate who was, by her own admission, not well-informed about the 1996 Clarification. We believe that Commissioners were thereby thwarted in their efforts to obtain the best information from the best sources.

- **The Commission had inadequate time for serious review.** Deadlines for Commission consideration of issues and decision-making did not allow Commissioners to do the kind of careful study warranted by the issues. For example, Commissioners had only six working days after the last public hearing to list and explain each of their proposed recommendations. Commissioners also had only two working days before the final decision-making meeting in Washington, D.C. to review the first draft of the proposed report. Commissioners were given less than a week to respond to the final draft of the report. We specifically urged another meeting of the full Commission to carefully review the language and impact of the final report, to no avail.

- **The Commission was not provided information on, nor therefore was able to consider, the impact of its recommendations.** The Commission was not provided with any data on the effect of its recommendations, including their impact on participation opportunities and scholarships for female athletes. Additionally, recommendations to change the 1996 Clarification were made without an accommodation to the Commissioners who requested, on several occasions, to circulate and discuss the extensive guidance provided in that Clarification. Commissioners were told that there was insufficient time for this type of analysis.

- **The arrangements made for expression of minority views were insufficient.** The Commission authorized inclusion of short statements of minority views following the recommendations on which there was dissent, but did not allow for any fuller statement of the dissenters' rationales or inclusion of concerns about the drafting of other portions of the report. As a result, the report does not reflect a full statement of the views of each of the Commissioners.

CONCLUSION

Equal opportunity for women and girls in education is of the utmost importance to our nation. The opportunity to participate in athletics is a critical component of that equality, since it opens the door for millions to play sports, receive college scholarships and obtain other important benefits—including increased health, self-esteem, academic performance, responsible social behaviors and leadership skills—that flow from sports participation.

Women and girls have made substantial strides toward equality in the 30 years since Title IX was passed. There is much more to be done, however, before Title IX's goals are achieved. Those goals are too important to be compromised by any weakening of the policies that have promoted the advances that have occurred or by anything less than the strongest enforcement of current law.

For these reasons, we ask the Secretary specifically to reject Recommendations 12, 14, 15, 17, 18, 19, 20, 23 and the unnumbered proposal in the majority report and to keep current policies in place without change. Rather than changing the policies that have been so important in opening opportunities for women and girls—when their job is not yet done and when their validity has been consistently upheld—the Department of Education should focus on using those policies to educate schools and the public about the importance of equal opportunity, the need to keep working to achieve it, and the flexibility of the means by which schools can provide it. Women and girls who play sports—and the fathers and brothers who support them—deserve no less.

Notes

1. Department of Health, Education and Welfare, *Policy Interpretation,* 44 Fed. Reg. At 71419 (1979).
2. U.S. General Accounting Office, No. 01–297, *Intercollegiate Athletics: Four-Year Colleges' Experiences Adding and Discontinuing Teams* (hereafter "GAO Report"), March 2001, at 7.
3. National Federation of State High School Associations (NFHS), *2001 High School Athletics Participation Survey.*
4. NCAA, *Gender Equity Report* (2000) at p. 20.
5. See NCAA, *Gender Equity Report* (2000), tables at pp. 16, 28, 40, 52, 64.
6. See, e.g., Teegarden, Proulx, et al., *Medicine and Science in Sports and Exercise,* Vol. 28 (1996), pp. 105–13 (citing health benefits); D. Sabo, et al., *The Women's*

Sports Foundation Report: Sport and Teen Pregnancy (1998) (adolescent female athletes have lower rates of sexual activity and pregnancy); NCAA,'"Study on Graduation Rates," in *NCAA News* (June 28, 1995) (female student-athletes have higher grades, are less likely to drop out, and have higher graduation rates than their non-athletic peers).

7. *Game Face,* "From the Locker Room to the Boardroom: A Survey on Sports in the Lives of Women Business Executives," Feb. 2002.

8. *Cohen v. Brown University,* 101 F.3d 155, 178–79 (1st Cir. 1996), *cert. denied,* 520 U.S. 1186 (1997).

9. GAO Report. Data include both NCAA and NAIA institutions, thereby eliminating double counting schools with dual NAIA and NCAA memberships.

10. NCAA, *1982–2001 Sports Sponsorship and Participation Statistics Report,* p. 119.

11. GAO Report at p. 14.

12. *See Chalenor v. University of North Dakota,* 2002 U.S. App. LEXIS 14404 (8th Cir. May *30,* 2002); *Pederson v. Louisiana State University,* 213 F.3d 858, 879 (5th Cir. 2000); *Neal v. Board of Trustees of The California State Universities,* 198 F.3d *763,* 770 (9th Cir. 1999); *Homer v. Kentucky High School Athletic Association,* 43 F.3d 265, *274–75* (6th Cir. 1994); *Kelley v. Board of Trustees, University of Illinois, 35* F.3d 265, 270 (7th Cir. 1994). *cert. denied,* 513 U.S. 1128 *(1995); Cohen v. Brown University,* 991 F. 2d 888 (1st Cir. *1993),* and 101 F.3d *155,* 170 (1st Cir. 1996), *cert. denied,* 520 U.S. 1186 (1997) (this case was before the First Circuit twice, first on Brown University's appeal of a preliminary injunction granted by the district court, and the second time after a trial on the merits); *Roberts v. Colorado State Board of Agriculture,* 998 F.2d 824, 828 (10th Cir. 1993), *cert. denied,* 510 U.S. 1004 (1993); *Williams v. School District of Bethlehem,* 998 F.2d 168, 171 *(3d Cir. 1993).*

13. *Neal v. Board of Trustees of The California State Universities,* 198 F.3d 763, 770 (9th cir. 1999) (emphasis added).

14. GAO Report at p. 14

15. GAO Report at p. 12.

16. U.S. Department of Education, Clarification of Intercollegiate Athletics Policy Guidance: The Three-Part Test, at p. 3.

17. NCAA Gender Equity Report, 1999–2000, at p. 15.

18. Welch Suggs, "Getting Ready for the Next Round," *The Chronicle of Higher Education,* Vol 49, Issue 23, p. A39 (Feb. 14, 2003).

19. The Commission's report suggests that non-traditional students are those over the age of 32. We assume that this is a typographical error, since the Commission clearly intended to exclude those who are "older than the traditional, full-time undergraduate college athlete," and specifically defined those students as students over the age of 24 in the draft report that the majority approved.

20. U.S. Department of Education, National Center for Education Statistics, *http://nces.ed.gov/pubs2002/digest2001/tables/dt174.asp.*

21. *Cohen v. Brown University,* 101 F.3d 155, 178–79 (1st Cir. 1996), *cert. denied, 520* U.S. 1186 (1997).

4

Testimony at the
Chicago Town Hall Meeting

Katherine Kersten

On September 17, 2002, the Commission on Opportunity in Athletics held the second of four public meetings to hear testimony about Title IX and its current enforcement mechanisms. One of the panelists at the meeting, held in Chicago, was Katherine Kersten, senior fellow for cultural studies at The Center of the American Experiment in Minneapolis, MN. According to Ms. Kersten, the "proportionality" test—currently used to determine compliance under Title IX—is a gender quota of the kind that the language of Title IX specifically rejects. In her view, the proportionality test needlessly limits male students' athletic opportunities. Ms. Kersten recommended that the Commission use statistical analysis to determine whether factors like campus demographics or differences in student interest—rather than discrimination—account for numerical disparities in men's and women's participation in college sports.

On January 31, 2003, the Commission released its report to Secretary of Education Rod Paige. Among other things, the report recommended that the Department of Education consider permitting colleges to use interest surveys as part of their planning for athletics. However, on February 28, 2003, Secretary Paige rejected this recommendation, along with all other recommendations that the commissioners did not approve by unanimous vote. As a result, the Department will likely continue to use the proportionality test as a primary means of judging compliance under Title IX. Ms. Kersten's testimony—a critique of the proportionality test—is thus of continued relevance, and appears below.

Title IX prohibits sex discrimination in all aspects of education. So how are girls and boys faring—relative to one another—in American schools today?

There are striking gender disparities. And they are repeated, in one form or another, in schools all across America. Generally, however, these disparities don't favor boys, but girls.

On average, American boys' academic performance is well below girls'. For example, in Edina, MN—the Twin Cities suburb where I live—girls are 67 percent of top-ranked students, and earn 65 percent of A's and 59 percent of B's. Boys, on the other hand, are 75 percent of special education students, and 90 percent of students who are suspended or otherwise disciplined. Boys' relatively poor academic performance is a major reason for the growing gender gap in college attendance. Today, 57 percent of college students are female, and 43 percent are male. The gap is expected to widen in the future.

Girls also dominate in most high school extracurricular activities. Nationally, they are 70 percent of students in vocal music, 64 percent of those in orchestra, and 61 percent of those in speech and drama. They also outnumber boys in activities like yearbook, honor society, and student government.

What causes these disparities? If we applied the proportionality test used in connection with Title IX, our analysis would be simple. We'd compare the percentage of girls and boys in orchestra (64 percent vs. 36 percent) with student enrollment (50 percent/50 percent) and con-clude that sex discrimination—specifically, antimale bias—is to blame. But as we all know, no one thinks of looking at the matter this way. The reason is that American parents and educators know that the world is much more complex than this analysis suggests. Parents who learn that boys are 90 percent of students suspended know that boys have a greater tendency than girls to engage in rowdy behavior. My own son isn't in orchestra or French Club, but not because bias keeps him out. His interests are playing basketball and soccer, and playing drums in his rock band.

Here's the point. Today, there are many gender gaps in American educational institutions, but there's only one situation where statistical disparities are automatically assumed—as a matter of policy, and with no further proof—to be due to illegal sex discrimination. That area is college sports, as governed by the proportionality test of Title IX.

The proportionality test purports to be a test of gender fairness. But its logic rests on one critical (and dubious) assumption: that males and females—at every college in the nation—have an equal desire to play competitive team sports. The key word here is "equal"; it's clear that tens of thousands of women do want to play. But are women, as a group, interested enough in intercollegiate sports to make strict proportionality the standard of fairness and equal access? If the answer is no, the proportionality test has no basis in logic.

There is significant evidence that women, as a group, have less interest in collegiate sports than men, in part because they have broader extracurricular interests. This evidence comes from many sources, including SAT interest surveys, sports participation rates at all-women's schools, and women's participation rates in intramural and community sports programs.

The reason we're here today is that opponents of the proportionality test claim that many schools have discriminated against men—by cutting male teams and roster sizes—in an effort to comply with that test's numerical balance requirements. Now, advocates of the proportionality test make several arguments in favor of Title IX's current enforcement mechanism. Initially, some of these seem plausible, but it's important to examine closely their basis in fact.

- The first claim is that the proportionality test is only one of three "prongs" of the regulatory test for compliance with Title IX, and that schools are free to choose whichever form of the test they prefer. But in reality, things don't work this way. Proportionality—with its gender quotas—is the only "safe harbor" for schools that wish to avoid costly, time-consuming investigations and lawsuits. Prongs II and III are merely temporary measures on the way to full compliance, and invite future lawsuits.
- Proportionality advocates' second claim is that men's teams and opportunities have actually increased, not decreased, since Title IX was adopted. Advocates point to NCAA and GAO studies that purportedly show an increase in men's opportunities since 1981. In fact, however, over the period those studies cover, many new colleges joined the NCAA and the NAIA, and brought their existing men's teams with them. As a result, the appearance of expanded male opportunity is illusory. In 1985, there were 253 male athletes per NCAA campus. In 2001, there were 199.
- Proportionality advocates' next claim is that athletic opportunities for college women remain in short supply. In fact, however, in 2001 the

NCAA had 582 more women's teams than men's teams, and in most sports, women's teams were entitled to more scholarships than men's teams.

- Advocates' fourth claim is that Title IX, as currently enforced, is not fundamentally about numbers—that is, gender quotas—but about budgets. "If only that stubborn school would cut its football budget," they say, "it could comply with Title IX." Again, the reality is different. The proportionality test clearly focuses not on budgets, but on numbers of athletes by sex. That's why, in an effort to comply, some schools have cut men's teams even though donors have offered to underwrite those teams' costs completely. Men must go, to bring male/female numbers into balance.

- Proportionality advocates also claim that most colleges—72 percent to be precise—have managed to comply with Title IX without cutting men's teams. But colleges that haven't yet cut teams may have to do so tomorrow. Title IX is a moving target, especially as female enrollment climbs. The most common mechanism that schools use to reach proportionality without cutting men's teams is rigorous roster management—a process largely invisible to outsiders. Today, schools routinely cap participation on male teams, often at levels well below what's required to build a competitive squad. They also prohibit male walk-ons, thus withholding the chance to participate from athletes who cost the school next to nothing, and play only for the love of the game.

- Finally, advocates of proportionality point to football as a primary culprit in blocking Title IX compliance. However, at many big football schools, football is the goose that laid the golden egg—it helps finance women's sports. Two recent studies show that women's sports are strongest at schools where football makes money. The fact is, though some proportionality advocates may not approve, American sports fans love football. At many large schools, football games attract thousands of alumni and potential donors to the campus, with results that benefit everyone. Proportionality advocates frequently point to football "excesses" like training tables, and hotel stays before home games to keep players away from dorm noise and distractions. At the University of Minnesota, dropping these would save about $50,000 annually—a sum that wouldn't begin to cover the costs of a new women's sports team. I do think, however, that proposals to address football coaches' salaries deserve serious study.

This is how the data on Title IX look to me, but others obviously see things differently. How is the commission to sort through our varying interpretations? I encourage the commissioners to appoint a panel of social science experts to carry out a rigorous statistical analysis of the data at issue here. These data should be subjected to regression analysis—a tool that's become routine in legal cases involving charges of discrimination. Regression analysis can reveal whether factors like differences in student interest or campus demographics— rather than discrimination—account for numerical disparities. I suspect such analysis would reveal that proportionality is a relatively crude measure of gender fairness, which uses an essentially arbitrary benchmark.

One final thought. In recent years, all across the legal world, proportionality tests—like the one Title IX employs—have essentially been discredited. Whether the issue is school desegregation or college admissions or employment or housing, courts no longer presume discrimination simply on the basis of statistical disparities. As we revisit Title IX's enforcement mechanism, shouldn't we take this into account?

Today, Title IX is at a crossroads. For years, Americans have heard about the law's beneficial purposes and results. Now—for the first time—they are beginning to learn about the dark side of Title IX, as currently enforced. Americans prize their daughters' athletic opportunities, but they also prize their sons'. If proportionality begins to creep into high schools, I think it will meet very determined resistance. Americans believe in justice, fair play, and rewarding individual merit. In my view, Title IX's proportionality test flies in the face of all of these.

5

What To Do About Title IX

Andrew Zimbalist

In January 2002, the National Wrestling Coaches Association (NWCA) sued the U.S. Department of Education for the way in which its Office of Civil Rights (OCR) has implemented Title IX regulations and enforcement. Like other critics, the NWCA charges that Title IX regulations function as an illegal quota system. In order to meet the Title IX "quotas" for female athletes, the critics argue, schools have eliminated wrestling, gymnastics, and other men's sports to the detriment of gender fairness.

While it is true that the number of male wrestling and gymnastics teams has been sharply reduced since Title IX's passage in 1972, it is problematic to attribute these cuts to Title IX. The greatest drop in the number of men's wrestling teams occurred between 1982 and 1992, when it fell from 363 to 275. Similarly, during 1982–1992 men's gymnastics teams decreased from 79 to 40.

But over these years there was little enforcement of Title IX. From 1981 to 1984 the Reagan administration dragged its feet on gender equity, then Title IX was eviscerated by the 1984 Grove City Supreme Court decision. The Court held that only the particular college departments that received federal funds directly were subject to Title IX. Thus, if a college's athletic department did not receive direct federal assistance, it did not have to comply with Title IX.

This chapter is based on the oral and written testimony presented by the author before the U.S. Department of Education's commission on Title IX, San Diego, California, November 20, 2002.

The power of Title IX was not restored until 1988. In 1987, Congress passed the Civil Rights Restoration Act which asserted that if a college received federal assistance then all its departments were subject to Title IX. However, President Reagan vetoed the Act. It was not until Congress overrode the veto in 1988, that Title IX became a viable instrument to promote gender equity in college sports. Yet, Title IX enforcement languished during the George H. W. Bush administration and it was not until 1993 that it was vigorously implemented.

Why then did the number of men's wrestling and gymnastics teams drop so precipitously during 1982–1992? In the case of gymnastics the answer seems to be schools' concern with legal liability. Indeed, the number of female gymnastics teams lost during this period was 83, more than double the loss of 39 in male teams. Would anyone attribute the loss of women's teams to the enforcement of Title IX?

Some have suggested that the explanation for wrestling's decline, in part, is a decline in interest; perhaps as young men have shifted their allegiances to the two most rapidly growing sports, soccer and football.

The U.S. General Accounting Office issued a report (GAO–01–128) on gender equity in college athletics in December 2000. Considering all NCAA and NAIA institutions, the report found that the number of men's athletic teams increased by a net 36 between 1981 and 1999. The number of participation opportunities for men increased by 7,000 between 1981 and 2001.[1]

Women have made enormous gains but today they still represent only 41 percent of college athletes (despite the fact that women represent 56 percent of all college students) and, according to the last NCAA Revenues and Expenses study, in 2001 the average operating budget for men's sports in Division IA was $10.9 million while for women's sports it was $4.6 million.

The NWCA claim that Title IX represents a quota system is also misguided. Title IX implementation guidelines allow a college to be in compliance by meeting any one of three criteria (prongs). The first criterion alone is quantitative and states that the proportion of athletes must be substantially proportional to the share of students by gender. The second criterion states that a school must have a history of ongoing improvement with regard to the underrepresented gender. The third criterion is that a school can show it has effectively accommodated the interests and abilities of the discriminated sex. The possibility that a school can be in compliance by fulfilling either the second or third criterion—which are not quantitative—means that there is no quota system.

To be sure, the December 2000 GAO report on Gender Equity revealed that of the 74 Title IX cases considered by the Department of Education's OCR, in fully 49 of these the schools chose for their compliance to be evaluated by the third prong (full and effective accommodation). In another four cases, the schools' compliance was judged in accordance with prong two (continuing expansion). Thus, in 53 of the 74 cases (or 71.6 percent), the first prong (proportionality) was not applied.

In a November 13, 2000 letter to the GAO's Associate Director, OCR's Norma Cantu affirmed the continuation of this pattern: "In fact, most schools investigated by OCR have chosen to comply with Title IX using methods other than substantial proportionality. Thus, most schools are complying with Title IX by methods for which a comparison of the number of male versus female athletes is irrelevant."

The athletics' arms race is alive and well, but it has little to show for itself on the bottom line. The 2002 NCAA Revenues and Expenses study finds that of the 114 reporting DIA schools, the average athletic department deficit was $600,000 in 2001. If one adds to this the average $1.425 million in student fees going to athletics and the $4.625 million in donations going to athletics, the standalone athletic department operating deficit averages $6.05 million. Even this number substantially understates the average subsidy to intercollegiate athletics at DIA schools.

The problem is that the one-sided incentives in DIA lead most schools to chase the Holy Grail of financial gain. But, like the NCAA itself, athletic departments are run by ADs, coaches and conference commissioners who do not have to answer to stockholders and do not face the financial discipline of the marketplace. The consequence is endemic waste.

For example, DIA football does not need 85 scholarships. Sixty would do fine. NFL teams have 45 roster, plus seven reserve, players. The average Division IA team has 32 walk-ons plus 85 scholarship players. If football scholarships were cut to 60, the average college would save approximately $750,000 annually, enough to finance more than two wrestling teams (whose average cost is $330,000 per team).

College coaches have protested that college football teams cannot be properly compared to professional teams. The latter, they say, can always call up reserves when players get injured, but college teams must have players on their rosters. This is a red herring. The NCAA Injury Surveillance System Summary reports that for the 2000–2001 season the serious injury rate during games in football was 14.1 per 1000 athlete exposures, while the rate in football practices was 1.6 per 1000. If we assume that 60 players enter a game and the team plays 13 games during the year (i.e., including a postseason game), then the average total number of serious injuries (where a player is out seven or more days) from games is 11 per year. If on average each such player misses two games, then the average number of game-injured players is 1.69 per game.

Performing a similar computation for practice-injured players (assuming 80 exposures per practice, five practices per week and 15 weeks of practice) yields 9.6 injured players during the year. If each misses two games on average, then the average number of practice-injured players is 1.48 per game, and the total number of injured players per game is 3.17. To be cautious, one can even double or triple this estimate and there would be fewer than seven or fewer than ten injured players per game. There is no justification here for having 85 grants-in-aid for a Division IA football team, even if the average team did not have 32 walk-ons.

But why stop here? The NCAA should seek a congressional antitrust exemption with regard to coaches' salaries. Currently, there are dozens of Division I men's basketball coaches who make over $1 million and some who make over $2 million, and there are dozens more football coaches in this category. Knock them down to $200,000 (which would still put them above 99 percent of the faculty) and colleges would be able to add another three to six sports, or, heaven forbid, reduce their large athletic deficits. Lest anyone think that these stratospheric coaches' salaries are justified economically, let me remind you that economic theory predicts a coach will be paid a salary up to his marginal revenue product in a competitive labor market. That said, how can it be that the top-paid coaches in college football and men's basketball get comparable compensation packages to each other when the average DIA football team has revenues fully three times as high as the average DIA basketball team. And, how can it be that the top dozen or two DIA football coaches get paid salaries similar to the

NFL coaches, when the average NFL team has revenues more than ten times as high as the average DIA football team. These coaches' compensation packages have more in common with the bloated stock option plans in Enron, Worldcom, and other corporations than they do with a competitive marketplace.

Coaches are reaping part of the value that is produced by their unpaid athletes. If unpaid athletes are subject to a restraint of trade because they are amateurs, then Congress should be willing to allow coaches' salaries also to be restrained.

Other savings are available to athletic programs. Colleges going to bowl games might also consider reducing the size of their traveling entourages (Nebraska took a delegation of 826 to the Rose Bowl in 2001 and spent $2.3 million), eliminating the practice of putting the men's basketball and football teams up at a local hotel before home games, diminishing the size of coaching staffs, cutting the length of the playing season in many sports, and so on.

Let me conclude with a final comment about DIA football. One often hears that gender equity is fine, but football should be taken out of the equation. That is, remove football's 85 scholarships and its operating budget before judging parity between men and women's sports. There is no justification for such a policy. One might as well argue that women's crew should be taken out before the gender participation numbers are compared. Title IX does not state that there shall be no gender discrimination where revenue generation is equal. It simply states that there shall be no gender discrimination—period. A sport's presumed profitability is plainly not a relevant criterion. As stated in Article I of the NCAA Constitution, college sports are based on the principle of amateurism and the subordination of athletic to academic goals. As such, Division I and II schools benefit mightily from not directly paying their athletes, from tax exemptions on facility bonds and from special tax treatment of UBIT income. Further, in 1984 the Supreme Court determined that the NCAA may legitimately restrain trade in many areas because, *due to its amateur branding*, college sports increase output and enhance consumer welfare. If college sports were to professionalize and separate out their football programs, using non-matriculated athletes and paying them salaries and benefits, then there would be a case to eliminate football from gender equity reckonings. As long as football benefits from the umbrellas of amateurism and the academy, however, the only rational course is to treat it the same as all sports programs for Title IX purposes.

In sum, the financial problem with college sports today is not Title IX or its implementation guidelines. The problem is waste.

Note

1. As with all time trends, by carefully selecting a beginning and end point one can frequently argue that the trend line moves in either direction. For instance, if one uses 1971–1972 as the base year then the total number of male student-athletes falls from 248,000 to 237,000 (in 1998-99). Yet, if one uses 1976–1977 (before the OCR three-pronged test was promulgated), the number of male athletes rises from 236,000 to 237,000. Given the year-to-year fluctuations and other accounting issues, it seems reasonable to conclude that the total number of male college athletes has basically been flat over the last 35 years. In any event, it is clear that there are many influences other than Title IX behind these participation numbers. In its December 2000 study, the GAO stated (p. 22): "from the mid-1960s to the early 1970s, just before Title IX was enacted, men's annual participation rates in intercollegiate sports declined and women's participation rates rose. Changing social and cultural attitudes appear to have contributed to women's increased interest and participation in athletics before Title IX was passed."

6

Equal Opportunity in Education and Sport

Lisa Keegan

I've got to admit my crabbiness on this issue right up front; to admit otherwise would be unsportsmanlike. My frustration stems from the fact that sports, while important, are not something that all children must fundamentally engage in—but academics are. Therefore, the quest for equal participation in all competitive sports seems to me a distraction from a far more compelling, but related, struggle; namely, that while we have absolutely evolved in our expectation that sports will be available for both boys and girls, we have continued to accept as routine a system of education that regularly fails to provide equal opportunities for certain groups of our children.

I absolutely embrace the belief that all children can benefit from an involvement in sports, and my time on the Commission on Equal Opportunity in Sports has only reaffirmed my belief in the value of the participation of women in athletics. However, my interest in ensuring equal participation of the sexes in athletics is only a fraction of my conviction that all children—regardless of sex or race or anything else—must have an equal opportunity to learn at least the essential knowledge that will give them choices after high school. Without equal academic opportunities in elementary, middle, or high school, many students may never have the chance to succeed in life, much less at a sport.

Jealousy aside, I came away from my experience on the Commission convinced that we have made an incredible advance in providing opportunities for young women in sports and athletics. I have been and continue to be a firm believer in Title IX; but I am also painfully aware that our progress is largely a reflection of our evolving beliefs about what young women are capable of or even want to take part in. Here again, I envy the policy inherent in Title IX and its success. In the world I live in—the world of academic achievement—we have only just now seen a federal law approved that declares that our national academic aspirations apply to all students, not just to some.

The fact is that as a nation, we maintain certain beliefs, behaviors, and practices—and these convictions can change over time. In an admirable attempt to accelerate the practice of our new and improved beliefs, we pass laws that are meant to express the ideal condition for which we want to strive. Such legislative efforts are noble and necessary; they have been oft repeated in this nation, most often to our credit as a society. Unfortunately, the mere passage of a law does not automatically change all attitudes or shape all behavior. In the aftermath of passing a law, many of our institutions remain oriented toward achieving previous goals or meeting now obsolete priorities. In order to force any change of behavior where it is not evolving on its own, lawmakers demand that specific actions be taken when the law is ignored. This is called enforcement of the law—and it's where we meet the limits of our efforts.

While the enforcement of the law is meant to reiterate its broader mission, there is plenty of opportunity for mischief. The mischief is not due to lack of motivation or even the enforcement itself; rather, it is from the necessity of creating an "objective" way to measure compliance with the law. Objective enforcement is often far removed from the larger and loftier intentions of the law, and can sometimes lead to an independent series of burdensome regulations, onerous legal precedents, and a good share of folk-lore...all of which began with the intention of strengthening the existence of a law, then ended up making a mockery of its intention.

The flaws inherent in this "objective" approach to compliance haunt me. In reviewing the history of the incredibly important laws regarding access to public education, we can only reflect that while the law aspires to equal access to education, the "objective" enforcement of the law, at least up until last year, only required us to count the number and colors of students in a school. We assumed naively that if a campus had an equal representation of students of different sexes and colors, and each of those students had access to equal school facilities, then an equality of education would result. At least, most of us *believed* that this was the assumption, although looking at such a theory with a pragmatic eye makes one wonder how such an assumption was ever made. Incredibly enough, though, I have actually heard so-called "experts" argue that integration was in itself a sufficient goal—that is, that the mere proximity of a Black child to an Anglo child would somehow osmotically benefit the Black child, as if the white child would provide an inspiration of sorts. I choked when I first heard of such nonsense; I dislike rewriting it here. The fact remains that the laws regarding integration of schools sought to create real equal opportunity, not simply the *appearance* of equal opportunity. So while a bird flying over a schoolyard might remark on successful integration based on the number of children of different colors and sexes milling about on the playground, the cold reality is that if those children are not being challenged equally, then the goal of the law has been left behind.

The intentions of desegregation law remain beautifully powerful; the struggle remains the right struggle. But it is the precedent for the enforcement—that difficult objective enforcement—that has failed our children. A simple review of which students in an inner city magnet school are attending the international baccalaureate classes and which are in remedial math will convince us of that fact—odds are that the former is filled with white students, and the latter with minorities. Same school, different destinies, despite the numbers showing that the school was compliant and thus everything should have been equal. Equal educational opportunity must mean equal access to excellent instruction for every child—or it means nothing at all.

Likewise, in the battle to enforce Title IX, we do not review access to sports or participation generally; regulation for the sake of enforcement means we only count participation at the collegiate level, and then only in competitively ranked sports. Like that bird flying over a schoolyard, we're only looking to see who's in a particular arena and gauging success based on a headcount. Competitively ranked sports count; intramurals and club sports don't. Casual interest in a sport without a desire to compete in an NCAA event, or free participation in an unregulated sport . . . these don't count, either. Yet these all matter enormously to the question of whether or not our nation's aspirations for women and men to have equal access to sport have been achieved.

But they don't count. The rules by which we play the game of determining the success of Title IX don't allow us to include these in the mix.

These seem to me to be two sides of the same problem. In the case of Title IX, we actually have a law that has assisted in supporting a societal change quite well, but whose enforcement is based on an amazingly narrow set of data about participation in sports and athletics broken out by gender. The point is not that this is a bad exercise; it does in fact have value. The distortion comes from basing one's perception of reality on a view through a very narrow lens. One can miss quite a bit. As a member of the Commission, I was inundated with a staggering amount of statistics regarding participation by men and women in sports, and I constantly marveled at the incredibly small degree of variance in participation rates that members were prepared to wage rhetorical war over. We spent a tremendous amount of time reviewing statistics and hearing impassioned arguments about an issue that is important, but has taken on a heightened sense of immediacy with the public because of the sheer volume of discussion and the assumption that there is some inequity inherent in the system. The fact remains that you cannot look at the statistics and deny the progress that has been made in providing equal access to sports and athletics. Yet we still have too many people involved with the issue who are unable or unwilling to acknowledge how far we've come since the inception of Title IX. Meanwhile, in academics we get the opposite. We pay too little attention to what is perhaps our most important domestic issue, and when we do turn to focus on it, we have an unseemly readiness to blame any failure in the system on the participants themselves. The statistics for academic achievement by race are depressingly well differentiated; our national shame should be the fact that we can predict academic attainment by race and wealth. Yet in education circles, the first response is to blame the lack of success on something about the student—her gender, her race, or her parents' income. However, in athletics, we don't blame female athletes for the failure of the system to provide them with opportunities; we change the system. The same should hold true for an education system that fails to provide equal opportunities for any group.

If we look at the legal orders that have been imposed on school districts across the nation to enforce the policies of equal access—and the rate at which schools have complied with ensuring they have numbers on their side—one could take pride in the considerable progress that has been made since the inception of the law. There is much to be said for this; for it is a remarkable accomplishment. But again, the numbers themselves are meaningless without true opportunity. Regulations are being complied with, certainly—but it will take an entirely new set of laws and regulations to make that promise of our original aspirations meaningful. I sometimes fear we're taking the easy way out. We focus on what we can count, not on the broader reality we could see if we worked at it. When addressing gender equity in access to sports, we ignore realities of progress and argue over marginal differences in sports participation. Meanwhile, in the realm of academic achievement, we congratulate ourselves on moving children into schools that appear to offer equal opportunities, but then we fail to look at what they actually learn. We just count who they are, not what they know. It took far too long to realign our educational policy to the lofty goal of looking at equal achievement, but it was the right thing to do.

In the case of equal opportunities in sports and athletics, our national policy has reflected the national will, and no honest assessment of the current situation can deny our progress. The danger now comes in ignoring those facts and clinging to a focus on a narrow set of statistics that may advance a point of view, but don't reflect reality. That can only lead to distortions in perception and faulty policies down the road. The call here is to admit success, tailor the law and its enforcement to the broader realities of women in sports, and continue along this path. History suggests that a simplistic formula for "counting" what's equal too often ignores looking at what's true. Don't compromise the facts in the name of an agenda; the ones who are truly compromised are the women who've worked hard to compete, both in the classroom and on the field.

7

Title IX and the Problem of Gender Equality in Athletics

Kimberly A. Yuracko

Title IX of the Education Amendments of 1972 prohibits discrimination on the basis of sex in federally funded programs.[1] In 1979, the Office for Civil Rights (OCR) of the Department of Education, the agency charged with administering Title IX, issued a Policy Interpretation setting forth a three-prong test for Title IX compliance.[2] Although there are formally three possible ways to comply with Title IX's antidiscrimination mandate, compliance most often comes down to the first requirement—the proportionality requirement.[3] Under the proportionality requirement, a college can show that it is in compliance with Title IX by providing varsity athletic spots for female and male students in proportion to their numbers in the undergraduate student body. This means that if a college is made up of 50 percent female students and 50 percent male students, the school must allocate one-half of its varsity team positions to women and one-half of its varsity team positions to men.

The proportionality requirement has come under attack in recent years by male athletes who blame Title IX for cuts made to men's teams and by scholars who argue that proportionality unfairly favors women in the distribution of scarce varsity athletic resources.[4] In June 2002, the Secretary of the Department of Education announced the creation of the Commission on Opportunity in Athletics (the "Commission") charged with the mission of reevaluating Title IX's application to college athletics.[5] On February 26, 2003, the Commission issued its report, *"Open to All" Title IX at Thirty*, which offered twenty-three recommendations to the Secretary of Education regarding how the current enforcement of Title IX should be modified.[6] On July 11, 2003, the Department of Education issued a public letter effectively maintaining the three-prong test for Title IX compliance, but emphasizing that proportionality was not the only acceptable means of compliance.[7]

In this article, I will begin by explaining why it is so difficult to answer the question of what it means to distribute college varsity athletic positions in a way that does not discriminate on the basis of sex. I will argue that, in fact, there is no single answer to this question. I will also argue, however, that proportionality is the best instantiation of Title IX's antidiscrimination mandate, not because of any entitlement of college age women to these resources, but because of the effect a proportional distribution of resources has on the social development and self-conceptions of younger girls and boys.

This article will proceed as follows. First I will show that society's paradigmatic antidiscrimination law—Title VII's prohibition on race and sex discrimination in employment—is not transferable to the world of sex-segregated college athletics, and therefore provides no guidance as to what nondiscrimination means in this context. Then I will show that the alternative distributional model most often proposed by critics of the proportionality requirement—one which allocates varsity athletic spots based on some measure of female and male students' interest in athletics—is theoretically and practically incoherent. Next I will present a different nondiscrimination model—one based on ensuring that younger girls and boys are given the skills and resources they will need to compete later in life. I will argue that this nondiscrimination model properly shifts the focus away from the entitlements of college level students to the obligations society has toward younger girls and boys. I will show, however, that this model, at least when focused on the development of self-respect, does not provide significant guidance as to what allocation of resources is appropriate. Finally, in the last part of this paper, I will argue that proportionality is the best implementation of Title IX's antidiscrimination mandate because it furthers the spirit of gender equality underlying Title IX by encouraging society's girls, as well as its boys, to develop a particularistic set of highly valued traits and attributes.

The Paradigmatic Antidiscrimination Model

Most basically, a prohibition on sex discrimination means that individuals, regardless of their sex, must be treated the same with respect to some relevant criteria. What the relevant criteria are against which individuals may properly be judged and distinguished varies by context.

The paradigmatic antidiscrimination model in this country is Title VII's prohibition on race and sex discrimination in employment.[8] Title VII mandates a "meritocratic ideal" whereby jobs are awarded on the basis of relevant ability, not social status.[9] Simply put, Title VII's antidiscrimination mandate is satisfied when women and men compete directly against each other for the same jobs, and the jobs are awarded to those individuals who best perform some set of required job qualifications.

Although criticism of the proportionality requirement is often based on its failure to abide by Title VII's meritocratic model,[10] I will show in this section that this model does not in fact translate to the context of athletics because of the sex segregated nature of athletic teams. The only coherent way to translate Title VII's meritocratic antidiscrimination model to the context of college athletics would be to have women and men compete directly against each other for the same spots on the same sex-integrated teams. Women and men would be measured against the same unitary metric and positions on varsity athletic teams would be awarded based on their performance. However, in all likelihood, a straight translation of Title VII's antidiscrimination model to the world of college athletics would lead to an almost complete absence of women from the formally co-ed varsity athletic teams. Not surprisingly, virtually no one is advocating a move to gender-integrated athletic teams.[11]

Once sex-segregated athletic teams are accepted, though, a true merit-based distribution of athletic team spots becomes impossible. There is no way to do a true merit-based comparison between female and male athletes across sex-segregated teams. To make this difficulty clear, I will present the two most plausible ways in which one might try to do such a merit-based comparison and show the inadequacies of both.

First, one might try to compare women's and men's athletic ability levels by ranking them on sex-specific ordinal scales. For example, male basketball players would be ranked on a simple scale in which each player is placed above those other players he is better than and below those whom he is worse than. The qualitative difference in the ability levels of the players is not measured. The players are simply ranked relative to each other. Therefore, if Adam is a better basketball player than Barry, who is better than Carl, then these three are entitled to positions on the men's basketball team in this order of priority. All women players would be ranked on a similar ordinal scale. Assume Amy is better than Barbara, who is better than Cindy. They are entitled to positions on the women's basketball team in this order.

Moreover, according to this ordinal ranking model, Adam is considered to have the same level of ability as Amy, Barry as Barbara, and Carl as Cindy. Therefore, if positions are distributed based on the players' sex-relevant ability levels, Amy and Barbara are as entitled to positions on sex-segregated athletic teams, as are Adam and Barry. If a school has funding for only four varsity positions, two must go to Amy and Barbara, and two must go to Adam and Barry.

This model of associating ability with a simple ordinal ranking and distributing spots based on rank would lead to equal spots for women and men. If a school has money to fund fifty spots, the twenty-fifth ranked woman will be considered as deserving as the twenty-fifth ranked man.[12]

Distributing athletic spots according to an intra-gender ordinal ability ranking is, however, far from an ideal translation of the meritocratic antidiscrimination model of Title VII. An ordinal ranking of ability is an extremely poor surrogate for the measure of talent that is crucial to the award of jobs because an ordinal ranking of athletic ability tells us very little about how well any individual actually plays a particular sport. Even if athletic ability is sex relevant in a meaningful sense, a gender-specific measure of ability that is devoid of any qualitative ability dimension seems lacking.

For example, assume that virtually no men participate in or have interest in synchronized swimming. If we forced all men to take a synchronized swimming test we would still develop an ordinal ranking of male synchronized swimmers, though the quality of the swimming of those at the top of the ladder would be bad and not much better than the quality of the swimming of those at the bottom of the ladder. Moreover, most people would probably agree that the top men were in fact "worse" than the top women, even considering relevant gender differences. Yet according to the ordinal ranking model, the best male synchronized swimmers would be as entitled to varsity athletic spots and funding as would the best female synchronized swimmers because both groups would be considered equally able according to the ordinal rankings. In other words, although one could distribute varsity positions across sex-segregated teams based on a simple ordinal ranking of ability, this measure of ability bears virtually no resemblance to the qualitative concept of ability used to distribute rewards under the unitary meritocratic model of Title VII.

One could try to overcome the problems with the ordinal ranking system with a second model that compares women's and men's levels of athletic ability in a more qualitative sense. Instead of placing women and men on straight ordinal scales, the ability of female and male athletes could be gauged by measuring the degree to which they are better or worse than the mean player of either gender. In this way, the notion of how good a player is would have some qualitative dimension (relative to the mean), but the measure of quality would still be sex specific.

In fact, though, cross-gender comparisons of this sort are meaningless. Consider the following example. We might think that because more women participate in synchronized swimming than do men, they are more dispersed in their levels of ability than are men. That is, some women are very bad at synchronized swimming, but some are very good at it. Moreover, those who are very good are actually much better than those who are bad or average. In comparison, we might think that men are not very dispersed in terms of their level of synchronized swimming ability. Instead, because almost no men participate in synchronized swimming, we might think that they are all clumped together at approximately the same level of skill.

We could then compare ability across sex-segregated teams by looking at the degree to which each individual is better or worse than their gender-specific mean. For example, assume that Amy, as the best female synchronized swimmer in the country, is much better than the average female synchronized swimmer. However, Adam, as the best male synchronized swimmer, is not very much better than the average male synchronized swimmer. One's intuition might be that Amy is in some sense a "better" synchronized swimmer than Adam, and is therefore more entitled to a varsity athletic position. Although this intuition is appealing, there is actually no meaningful way to compare Amy and Adam's levels of ability when neither the scales nor the means against which they are measured are comparable. In other words, there is no way to meaningfully compare the qualitative abilities of female and male athletes when their abilities are assessed against wholly different scales.

As these examples show, it is extremely difficult, if not impossible, to compare female and male students' athletic ability when ability is measured on distinctly intra-gendered scales. There is no single obvious way to make such ability comparisons, and what is being compared is something very different than what is being compared under the traditional meritocratic model of Title VII. Therefore, Title IX's antidiscrimination mandate for college athletics cannot simply map onto and adopt the antidiscrimination model of Title VII. Title IX must, necessarily, find an alternative model for what it means to treat women and men equally in the context of athletics. I turn next to the alternative most often suggested by the critics of the proportionality requirement.

The Interest-Based Alternative

The most commonly proposed alternative to distributing varsity athletic positions based on the percentages of women and men in the undergraduate student body is to distribute athletic positions based on women and men's relative levels of interest in athletics.[13] According to this approach, varsity athletic positions should be allocated to women's and men's sex-segregated teams based on female and male students' relative levels of interest in athletics. This model—focused on ensuring that women and men are treated equally with respect to their interest, rather than their ability, in athletics—is problematic, however, for both theoretical and practical reasons.

From a theoretical standpoint, distributing scarce resources based on interest level is strange and atypical. While as a society we often distribute scarce resources based on merit, and we sometimes distribute them based on some measure of utility, we do not, as a general matter, distribute scarce resources based on individual interest levels. In the case of employment, for example, we require that jobs be awarded based on some measure of merit. An individual is not entitled to a job simply because she has an extremely high level of interest in it. Interest is a necessary, but insufficient condition for the award of a job. In the context of education, we sometimes distribute scarce resources based on some measure of utility or capacity to benefit. This is again distinct from a distribution based on interest. The Individuals with Disabilities Education Act ("IDEA"), for example, provides that additional educational resources should be given to disabled school children.[14] The Act is premised on the belief that handicapped children will benefit more from the infusion of resources than will nonhandicapped children, and that society as a whole will benefit more from the disproportionate distribution of resources to disabled children than from some other distribution scheme.[15] Thus, the motivation behind the IDEA, which focuses on the benefits that resources will bring to disabled children and to society as a whole, is unconcerned with the degree to which children are actually interested in the resources.

Not only is a distribution based on "interest" atypical generally, it is also not how varsity athletic positions are distributed. Individual students do not win varsity athletic team positions based on their relative levels of interest in these positions. As in the context of employment, interest is necessary but not sufficient to the award of varsity positions. The actual positions are awarded based on intra-group measures of merit.

The interest-based distribution proposal is strange, too, because it suggests that the numbers of spots available to elite female and male athletes should be determined by the levels of athletic interest expressed by the rest of the female and male student body. It is unclear why the interest levels of women and men in the student body at large should determine the relative number of spots that the elite athletes of each sex should then be able to compete for. There seems to be no good reason why the opportunities of elite athletes should be determined by how much the nonathletes of each sex at their school care about athletics.

From a practical perspective, a reliance on student interest levels is also problematic. As a general matter, it is clear that women's and girls' interest in athletics is highly mutable and is affected by the athletic opportunities made available to them at the elementary, high school, and college levels.[16] More specifically, at each college, student interest in athletics will be affected by the particular athletic opportunities that are available. Women who are athletically inclined are unlikely to attend a school that does not offer significant athletic opportunities for women, while the existence of athletic teams is likely to generate new interest among existing students. In addition, student interest levels will be markedly affected by the school's own recruiting efforts.[17] In other words, the interest level of a particular student body in athletics depends both on what athletic opportunities are already available at the school and on what students the university seeks to attract.

In sum, society's paradigmatic antidiscrimination model, that of Title VII, cannot help us determine what it means to treat women and men equally with respect to the distribution of varsity athletic positions. The dominant alternative model proposed by critics of the proportionality requirement—a distribution based on student interest levels—is both theoretically indefensible and practically unworkable.

A Different Nondiscrimination Model

Given the inadequacies discussed above, this section presents an alternative way to think about what nondiscrimination or fair treatment means in this context. While the previous two antidiscrimination models focused on the relative entitlements of college age women and men to varsity athletic resources, it may be that a better way to understand Title IX's nondiscrimination mandate is to focus on the effects that a particular distribution model has on younger girls and boys. In particular, this section presents the antidiscrimination model that is most prevalent in the context of education and is used to consider what it means for society to distribute valuable resources fairly to children.

In the context of education, the mandate to treat children equally means something very different from what it means with respect to adults in the workplace. In the context of employment, the prohibition on discrimination translates into a mandate for equal opportunity—all individuals must be given the chance to compete for jobs on the same terms. Jobs must be awarded based on some measure of relevant ability or merit. In the context of education, however, nondiscrimination translates into a mandate for equal opportunity of a very different sort. In the context of education, equality of opportunity requires that all children receive an adequate or fair chance to develop the essential skills they will need to compete successfully later in life. I call this the "tool-giving" model of equality of opportunity.

The premise of the tool-giving model is that in order for society to treat children fairly, schools must provide all children with necessary skill training and must "level the playing field" to some degree in order to allow disadvantaged children to compete more effectively. In other words, when people talk about ensuring that all children have equal educational opportunities, they do not mean that children should compete against each other for books and teacher attention. Instead, discussions about equality of opportunity in the context of education are discussions about ways to ensure that all children have some real chance to develop the skills they will need to compete with others later in life.[18]

The proportional allocation of college varsity athletic spots to female and male students would be justified by the tool-giving equality of opportunity model if proportionality were necessary to ensure that girls had the same opportunity to develop some essential skill that boys have. The most distinctly liberal version of this tool-giving argument is one that connects the proportional distribution of college varsity-level athletic positions with the development of self-respect for younger girls.[19] An adequate degree of self-respect is critical to individuals' ability to compete for social rewards and to direct the course of their lives. To the extent that proportionality of college varsity athletic positions is essential to younger girls' and boys' abilities to develop the same kind and degree of self-respect, then proportionality may be both justified and required by this tool-giving model.

There are three ways in which proportionality of college varsity athletic positions may be critical to younger girls' and boys' self-respect levels. First, one might argue that the proportionality requirement is justified by the tool-giving model of equality of opportunity because proportionality signals women's equal social worth, and girls' self-respect is mediated by the social status of their gender. Proportionality signals women's equal social worth, thereby giving girls access to the same feelings of group-based self-respect to which boys have access. Lack of proportionality, in contrast, signals women's lack of social status, thereby depriving girls of the same degree of group-based self-respect that is available to boys.

The problem with this version of the tool-giving argument is that even if one agrees that proportionality sends a message of women's equal social worth while nonproportionality sends a message of social inferiority, the conclusion regarding this message's impact on individual self-esteem is not empirically supported. Empirical tests do not show a connection between individual self-esteem and the social status of one's salient social groupings. Instead, empirical research suggests that individuals who are members of socially disadvantaged groups do not have measurably lower levels of overall or global self-respect than do members of nondisadvantaged groups.[20]

Second, one might argue that girls' and women's self-respect is affected by how fairly they feel authority figures treat them. If proportionality is currently perceived to be fair, then anything less than proportionality will impair girls' self-respect.

Empirical research suggests that individual self-esteem is indeed mediated by perceptions of how fairly one is treated by group authorities.[21] It is not clear, however, that proportionality is generally accepted as a fair distribution of athletic resources, particularly by boys and men. To the extent that boys perceive proportionality as unfair, their own self-respect may be harmed. It would defeat the basic goal of the tool-giving equality of opportunity model, which is to ensure that all children have a fair opportunity to develop the skills they will need to compete later in life, if girls' self-respect were protected only at the expense of boys'.

Finally, one could make an argument that is essentialistic rather than empirical. That is, one could make a pre-empirical argument that nonproportionality of varsity athletic spots stigmatizes and degrades girls in a way that necessarily undermines their self-respect (even if we do not have the empirical research to demonstrate the harm).[22] This is a parallel argument to the one some commentators believe underlies the Supreme Court's decision in *Brown v. Board of Education*. [23] Although the Supreme Court in *Brown* did cite social science evidence to support its conclusion that "[s]eparate educational facilities are inherently unequal," [24] some commentators argue that the social science evidence was mere window dressing and not the basis of the Court's decision.[25] They argue that the basis for the decision was instead the simple fact that "everyone knew" that racial segregation was stigmatic for African Americans. One could justify the proportionality requirement for college athletics based on a similar pre-empirical assertion that giving girls and women fewer athletic positions than boys and men simply must harm their self-esteem because of the message such treatment sends. The weakness with this argument, however, is that there does not seem to be nearly the same level of social consensus regarding the social meaning and psychological effect of a lack of athletic proportionality on girls that there was regarding the meaning and effect of school segregation on African American children at the time of *Brown.*

In sum, a tool-giving equality of opportunity model focused on younger girls and boys offers a useful framework for thinking about the nondiscrimination obligations Title IX imposes on colleges distributing varsity athletic opportunities. It properly shifts the focus away from the narrow entitlement claims of college age women and men to the broader obligations society has to distribute resources so as to provide younger girls and boys with similar life opportunities. Yet it is not clear, based on current psychological research, whether proportionality, or any other distribution scheme, is required by the narrow self-respect focused version of this tool-giving model.

An Argument for Proportionality

While the previous section shifted the focus of Title IX's nondiscrimination requirement to younger girls and boys, but was limited to the development of their self-respect, the present section shows that proportionality becomes the best instantiation of Title IX's nondiscrimination requirement when this focus is broadened beyond self-respect. Proportionality encourages young girls (as well as boys) to develop a particularistic set of skills and attributes that are widely socially valued (and have traditionally been encouraged in boys). In particular, the proportionality requirement encourages girls to develop a sense of their own bodily agency and develop a conception of themselves as agents in their social and physical world.

There are two ways in which proportionality encourages the development of these valued traits and attributes. First, proportionality encourages young girls to develop bodily agency and a conception of themselves as active agents in the physical world through its creation of athletic female role models for girls. All girls may derive indirect benefits from the college proportionality requirement as a result of the role-modeling effects of having relatively high profile college-level female athletes.

This role-model argument relies, at a general level, on a theory of social groups. It relies on a claim that, because of the salience of gender-group membership, girls respond differently when they see a woman doing something than they do when they see a man doing the same thing. Indeed, psychology research supports the proposition that people are more affected by the attitudes and behaviors of members of their group than they are by nonmembers.[26]

The benefits generally associated with female, athletic role-models are, at the most basic level, an improvement in girls' physical health by encouraging girls to participate in athletics and to develop physical skills and good health. However, the beneficial effects for girls of having female athletic role models may also be psychological. Female athletes give girls a vision of themselves and of their bodies that differs from the vision of themselves that they have when their dominant role-models are fashion models and movie stars. That is, female athlete role models allow girls to develop an alternative vision in their own mind of who and what they can become, and of what socially valued versions of themselves might look like.[27]

This role-modeling argument does not, from a purely logical perspective, call for proportionality of college varsity athletic spots. Even if the initial desire to subsidize college athletic role models for girls is driven by a desire to encourage young girls to participate in competitive athletics, it is not clear that proportionality, rather than just some critical mass of female athletes, is required. Indeed, as a theoretical matter, there does not seem to be any reason why proportionality, rather than a critical mass of varsity female athletes, is necessary to have the desired role-modeling effects. It may be, though, that proportionality makes sense as a pragmatic way to operationalize the desired role-modeling effects. Because we do not know how many female college athletes we actually need in order to have the desired role-modeling effects, proportionality makes sense as a pragmatic compromise.[28]

Second, proportionality may play a role in a larger process of cultural transformation. Proportionality may be justified not on the grounds that the policy itself changes the way girls think of themselves and act upon the world around them, or not only on those grounds, but on the grounds that proportionality is one key part in a larger project of cultural transformation that will encourage such changes.

Proportionality may be one part of a social reconstruction project aimed at changing the cultural meanings, or "tags," associated not only with competitive athletics but also with physical agency more generally.[29] Proportionality may encourage girls to think of themselves and their bodies in a different way by tagging competitive physical activity as equally female, rather than exclusively male. Proportionality may, therefore, be part of a larger project to change the social meaning attached to femaleness from passive beauty or sex object to strong physical agent. Indeed, as such a resocialization measure, Title IX has already been very successful. While men still dominate sports, in the years since Title IX's proportionality requirement was enacted, women and girls play sports, and indeed participate in the physical world, in a way and to a degree that was unheard of before 1972.[30]

In conclusion, I have argued in this paper that there is no clear answer to the question of what it means to distribute college varsity athletic opportunities so as not to discriminate on the basis of sex. Sports, because of their sex-segregated nature, are so different from our paradigmatic model of nondiscrimination provided by Title VII, that Title VII offers no useful guidance for what equality means in this context. The dominant alternative proposal to proportionality—distributing athletic positions based on the interest levels expressed by female and male students—is theoretically unjustifiable and practically problematic. Title IX's antidiscrimination mandate simply cannot be well or fully understood by focusing only on the purported entitlements of female and male college students.

I have tried, therefore, to shift the focus of the Title IX debate from what distribution of college resources is fair to college women and men to what distribution is fair to younger girls and boys more generally. I have argued that proportionality is in fact the best instantiation of Title IX's nondiscrimination mandate because proportionality encourages girls to develop the same socially valued traits and attributes that society has long encouraged boys to develop. Proportionality provides girls with a set of alternative (and socially valued) viable conceptions of themselves both through the role-modeling effects of having visible college varsity female athletes, and more indirectly, by helping to change the social meanings attached to athleticism specifically, and physical agency more generally. In short, proportionality is the best interpretation of nondiscrimination in the context of college athletics because it encourages young girls (in addition to young boys) to develop a set of traits, skills, and possible self-conceptions that are widely considered to be important both for future success, and, more generally, for a good human life.

Notes

1. Title IX provides: "No person in the United States shall, on the basis of sex, be excluded from participation in, be denied the benefits of, or be subjected to discrimination under any education program or activity receiving Federal Financial assistance." 20 U.S.C. §1681(a)(2000).

2. Under the Policy Interpretation a school can show it is in compliance with Title IX if it can prove: 1) that it provides athletic opportunities for its female and male students in numbers substantially proportionate to their enrollments in the undergraduate student body; 2) that it has a history and continuing practice of program expansion for members of the underrepresented sex; or 3) that it has fully and effectively accommodated the interests and abilities of members of the underrepresented sex. See U.S. Dep't of Educ., Office for Civil Rights, *Title IX 1979 Policy Interpretation*, available at *http://www.ed.gov/offices/OCR/docs/t9interp.html.*

3. Compliance most often comes down to the proportionality requirement for two reasons. First, in light of the thirty years since Title IX's passage, it is difficult for any college to boast a history and continuing practice of program expansion for women if the school still does not provide proportional opportunities for women and men. Second, any time female students bring a Title IX lawsuit arguing that they are entitled to have a particular athletic team funded, it is difficult for a college to defend its lack of proportional opportunities by arguing that it has fully accommodated women's interests and abilities.

4. See National Wrestling Coaches Association Lawsuit, available at *http://www.nwcaadmin. bluestep.net.* See also William E. Thro & Brian A. Snow, "The Conflict Between the Equal Protection Clause and *Cohen v. Brown University*," 123 *Educ. L. Rep.* 1013, 1025 (1998) (arguing that the proportionality requirement violates the equal protection clause); Brian A. Snow & William E. Thro, "Still on the Sidelines: Developing the Non-Discrimination Paradigm under Title IX," 3 *Duke J. Gender L. & Pol'y* 1, 15–17 (1996) (describing the proportionality requirement as requiring quotas); Earle C. Dudley, Jr. & George Rutherglen, "Ironies, Inconsistencies, and Intercollegiate Athletics: Title IX, Title VII, and Statistical Evidence of Discrimination," 1 *Va. J. Sports & L.* 177, 213–14 (1999) (arguing that Title IX's proportionality requirement is an impermissible form of affirmative action imposing on universities an obligation to compensate for "societal discrimination").

5. See Valerie Strauss & Mike Allen, "Panel Named to Study Title IX: Law's Fairness to be Examined," *Wash. Post*, June 28, 2002, at A27.

6. The Commission's report is available at *http://www.ed.gov/inits/commissionsboards/athletics/.* Among the Commission's recommendations were the following. A recommendation that the OCR "should study the possibility of allowing institutions to demonstrate that they are in compliance with the third part of the three-part test by comparing the ratio of male/female athletic participation at the institution with the demonstrated interests and abilities shown by regional, state, or national youth or high school participation rates or national governing bodies, or by the interest levels indicated in surveys of prospective or enrolled students at the institution" (Recommendation 19, unanimously approved). A recommendation that "[t]he designation of one part of the three-part test as a 'safe harbor' should be abandoned in favor of a way of demonstrating compliance with Title IX's participation requirement that treats each part of the test equally. In addition, the evaluation of compliance should include looking at all three parts of the test, in aggregate or in balance, as well as individually" (Recommendation 21, unanimously approved). A recommendation that "[a]dditional ways of demonstrating equity beyond the existing three-part test should be explored by the Department of Education" (Recommendation 23, unanimously approved).

7. See July 11, 2003 "Dear Colleague" letter from Gerald Reynolds, Assistant Secre-

tary for Civil Rights at *http://www.ed.gov/offices/OCR/title9guidanceFinal.html* (last visited July 23, 2003).

8. Title VII provides: "It shall be an unlawful employment practice for an employer—(1) to fail or refuse to hire or to discharge any individual, or otherwise to discriminate against any individual with respect to his compensation, terms, conditions, or privileges of employment, because of such individual's race, color, religion, sex or national origin." 42 U.S.C. §2000e–2.

9. See Daniel A. Farber & Suzanna Sherry, "Is the Radical Critique of Merit Anti-Semitic?" 83 *Cal. L. Rev.* 853, 858 (1995) (explaining that "[t]he meritocratic ideal is that positions in society should be based on the abilities and achievements of the individual rather than on characteristics such as family background, race, religion or wealth").

10. See Eugene G. Bernardo, II, "Unsportsmanlike Conduct: Title IX and *Cohen v. Brown*," 2 *Roger Williams Univ. L. Rev.* 305, 349 (criticizing the *Cohen* court's adherence to the proportionality requirement on the grounds that "[d]espite the glaring similarity in phrasing and legislative intent, the *Cohen* courts have refused to adopt the Title VII-Title IX parallel and to follow the former's case law"); Walter B. Connolly, Jr. and Jeffrey D. Adelman, "A University's Defense to a Title IX Gender Equity in Athletics Lawsuit: Congress Never Intended Gender Equity Based on Student Body Ratios," 71 *Univ. of Detroit Mercy L. Rev.* 845, 862 (1994) (criticizing the proportionality requirement for tying Title IX liability to comparisons of women's athletic participants with the number of women in the student body rather than with the "qualified pool" of female students in keeping with the model for liability established by Title VII cases); Ross A. Jurewitz, "Playing at Even Strength:"Reforming Title IX Enforcement in Intercollegiate Athletics," 8 AM. *U. J. Gender Soc. Pol'y & L.* 283, 384 (complaining that "[a]lthough Title IX is significantly patterned after Title VII and other civil rights amendments, the courts have refused to look to Title VII's case law for jurisprudential guidance"); Earl C. Dudley, Jr. and George Rutherglen, "Ironies, Inconsistencies, and Intercollegiate Athletics: Title IX, Title VII, and Statistical Evidence of Discrimination," 1 *Va. J. Sports & L.* 177, 207–09 (1999) (arguing that Title IX should follow Title VII case law for how to establish discrimination based on statistics); Michael Straubel, "Gender Equity, College Sports, Title IX and Group Rights: A Coaches' View," 62 *Brook. L. Rev.* 1039, 1067–69 (1996) (criticizing the proportionality requirement for its failure to follow the model for liability established by Title VII).

11. Indeed, the Commission on Equality in Athletics apparently did not even consider such a possibility. See Commission Report, *supra* note 6. The few commentators who criticize sex-segregated teams do so not as part of an argument that the proportionality requirement is unfair to male students but instead as part of an argument that sex segregation stigmatizes women. Even these critics, though, still favor the maintenance either temporarily or permanently of some exclusively female teams in order to ensure that female students are not excluded wholly from competitive play. See Jessica E. Jay, "Women's Participation in Sports: Four Feminist Perspectives," 7 *Tex. J. Women & L.* 1, 21 (1997) (arguing that sex-segregated teams are based on stereotypes of female inferiority and harm women psychologically, socially, and occupationally); Karen L. Tokarz, "Separate But Unequal Educational Sports Programs: The Need for a New Theory of Equality," 1 *Berkeley Women's L.J.* 201, 232 (1985) (arguing that "[t]he major premise of segregation in sports on the basis of sex is the inherent inferiority of females as

actors. Segregation and exclusion of females from full participation in educational sports programs on the basis of average sex differences, rather than skill, imposes sex role stereotypes on females, inhibits their learning, denies them socially important status as school athletes, deprives them of opportunities for public exposure and prestige, reduces possibilities for them to obtain financial aid to college, and forecloses employment opportunities").

12. Of course, this model will not lead to a proportional division of spots in cases where women and men are not equally represented within the student body. Because a female student will always be considered as able as her similarly ranked male counterpart, athletic spots will always be distributed equally to female and male students regardless of whether the female to male ratio in the student body is 50–50 or 70–30.

13. Critics of the proportionality requirement often argue that varsity athletic positions should be distributed based on female and male students' relative levels of athletic interest and ability. Since I have already shown that it is meaningless to try to compare women's and men's athletic ability across sex-segregated teams, I focus here on the argument that spots should be distributed based on comparative levels of interest. See Bernardo, *supra* note 10, at 350 (arguing that discrimination should be found under Title IX only if female students are underrepresented on varsity athletic teams given the percentage of women in the group of students who are interested in and able to play varsity athletics); Jurewitz, *supra* note 10, at 348–49 (arguing that Title IX should find liability only if women are underrepresented in varsity athletics given their percentage in the qualified applicant pool—those students interested in and qualified to compete in intercollegiate athletics); Thro & Snow, "The Conflict Between the Equal Protection Clause and *Cohen v. Brown University,*"*supra* note 4, at 1028–29 (arguing that the proportionality requirement violates the equal protection clause because it does not distribute rewards based on individual interest and ability).

14. 20 U.S.C. §§1400–1491o (2000).

15. See Martin A. Kotler, "The Individuals with Disabilities Education Act: A Parent's Perspective and Proposal for Change," 27 *U. Mich. J.L. Reform* 331, 339 & n. 28 (1994); *Polk v. Central Susquehanna Intermediate Unit* 16, 853 F.2d 171 (3d Cir. 1998); Kimberly A. Yuracko, "One for You and One for Me: Is Title IX's Sex-Based Proportionality Requirement for College Varsity Athletic Positions Defensible," 97 *Nw. U.L. Rev.* 731, 764–65 (2003).

16. Female students' participation in high school interscholastic athletics increased from fewer than 300,000 in 1971 to more than 2.6 million in 1998–1999. Nat'l Fed'n of State High Sch. Ass'ns, Summary of Athletic Participation Totals by School Year, at *http://www.nfhs.org/Participation/Sports%20Participation%2701-FINAL.pdf* (last visited Jan. 12, 2003); Nat'l Fed'n of State High Sch. Ass'ns, Annual Sports Participation Survey: High School Participation (Univ. of Iowa Gender Equity in Sports Project ed.) [hereinafter High School Participation Survey], at *http://bailiwick.lib.uiowa.edu/ge/statistics.htm#220* (last visited Jan. 12, 2003). Female students' participation in intercollegiate athletics increased from 32,000 female athletes in 1971 to 150,000 in 1998–1999. *See* Nat'l Collegiate Athletic Ass'n, 1998–99 Participation Study—Women's Sports, at *http:// www.ncaa.org/participation_rates.*

17. Courts generally recognize the instability of existing athletic interests among a college student body. See *Neal v. Bd. of Trustees*, 198 F.3d 763, 769 n. 4 (9th Cir. 1999) ("[T]he creation of additional athletic spots for women would prompt universities to recruit more female athletes, in the long run shifting women's demand

curve for sports participation. As more women participated, social norms discouraging women's participation in sports presumably would be further eroded, prompting additional increases in women's participation levels."); see also *Cohen v. Brown University*, 101 F.3d 155, 177 (1st Cir. 1996) (stating that because of the existence of sex-segregated teams "and because recruitment of interested athletes is at the discretion of the institution, there is a risk that the institution will recruit only enough women to fill positions in a program that already under represents women, and that the smaller size of the women's program will have the effect of discouraging women's participation"); *Cook v. Colgate Univ.*, 802 F. Supp. 737, 746 (N.D.N.Y. 1992), *vacated as moot*, 992 F.2d 17 (2d Cir. 1993) (rejecting Colgate's argument that female students lacked sufficient interest and ability to field a varsity ice hockey team as pretext and finding that Colgate could recruit a competitive team of players from Canada and the northeastern United States).

18. Indeed, the tool-giving version of equality of opportunity dominates social and political discussions regarding educational resource allocations. See Yuracko, *supra* note 15, at 773.

19. This version of the tool-giving model of equality of opportunity is liberal because self-respect is a commonly accepted liberal good. Encouraging the development of self-respect does not violate the liberal commitment to value neutrality toward different conceptions of the good life because self-respect is essential in order for an individual to achieve her ends, whatever they may be. See John Rawls, *A Theory of Justice* 440 (1971). See also Cass Sunstein, "The Anticaste Principle," 92 *Mich. L. Rev.* 2410, 2430 (1994).

20. See Jennifer Crocker & Brenda Major, "Social Stigma and Self-Esteem: The Self-Protective Properties of Stigma," 96 *Psychol. Rev.* 608 (1989) (finding that the research "conducted over a time span of more than twenty years, leads to the surprising conclusion that prejudice against members of stigmatized or oppressed groups generally does *not* result in lowered self-esteem for members of those groups"); see also Tom Tyler et al., "Understanding Why the Justice of Group Procedures Matter: A Test of the Psychological Dynamics of the Group-Value Model," 70 *J. Personality & Soc. Psychol.* 913, 926 (1996) ("Social identity theory predicts that people's senses of self-worth are affected by their evaluations of the groups to which they belong. Unfortunately, related empirical research has not consistently supported this hypothesis."). Of course, these current empirical findings that the social status of one's group does not affect individual levels of self-respect are open to challenge. It might be that these calculations of self-respect are either mismeasurements, or are not measuring the kind of self-respect about which we are concerned. Indeed Crocker and Major suggest that part of the reason that members of stigmatized groups may not express lower levels of self-esteem than members of nonstigmatized groups is precisely because they make in-group rather than out-group comparisons—they compare themselves to other similarly stigmatized individuals whose outcomes are also relatively poor, thereby making their own accomplishments appear more favorable. If what society really cares about is a measure of self-respect in which members of socially-disadvantaged groups are pushed to compare and measure themselves against members of more advantaged groups, then the current empirical studies may not be testing the kind of self-respect with which we are truly concerned.

21. See Tyler et al., *supra* note 20 at 927 (explaining that "[f]air and respectful treatment by authorities who represent important groups communicates feelings of respect and pride. Feelings of respect and pride, in turn, are related to self-esteem, feelings of obligation to group authorities, and the desire to help the

group beyond what is required"); see also Gerda Koper et al., "Procedural Fairness and Self-Esteem," 23 *Eur. J. Soc. Psychol.* 313 (1993) (finding that perceptions of procedural unfairness lowers individual self-esteem).

22. I take it that some version of this argument is behind Lucy Danziger and Jane English's arguments about the importance of visible elite female athletes. See Lucy Danziger, "Conclusion: A Seismic Shift in the Culture," in *Nike Is a Goddess: The History of Women in Sports* 313, 317 (Lisa Smith, ed., 1998) ("What happens among talented sportswomen at the elite levels makes its way into the culture. It's our version of the trickle-down concept: when women get paid to play basketball in front of 17,000 spectators, the rest of us, contenders in our own world of sports, feel a little bit more legitimate and take our pursuits more seriously."); Jane English, "Sex Equality in Sports," 7 *Phil. & Pub. Affairs* 269, 273 (1978) ("When there are virtually no female athletic stars or when women receive much less prize money than men do, this is damaging to the self-respect of all women. Members of disadvantaged groups identify strongly with each others' successes and failures. If women do not attain roughly equal fame and fortune in sports, it leads both men and women to think of women as naturally inferior.").

23. *Brown v. Bd. of Educ.*, 347 U.S. 483 (1954).

24. *Id.* at 495.

25. Edmond Cahn, for example, argues that it is a mistake to think that the Court in *Brown* based its decision on social science evidence rather than on a pre-empirical truth about the psychological harms of segregation. See Edmond Cahn, "Jurisprudence," 30 *N.Y.U. L. Rev.* 150, 157–60 (1955). Cahn contends that *Brown* was based on the essentially pre-empirical fact that the Court, and almost everyone else recognized, that segregation causes stigma and psychological harm to African Americans. *Id.* at 159. Similarly, Jack Greenberg, who argued part of the *Brown* case before the Supreme Court, contends that the Court simply used the scientific evidence to corroborate what it already knew about the meaning and impact of segregation. See Richard Sobel, "A Colloquy with Jack Greenberg About Brown: Experiences and Reflections," 14 *Const. Comment.* 347, 355 (1997).

26. See Marilynn Brewer & Rupert Brown, "Intergroup Relations," in *2 Handbook of Social Psychology* 554, 559 (Daniel T. Gilbert et al., eds., 1998) (explaining that "[i]ngroup membership [of which gender is one kind] is more than mere cognitive classification; it carries emotional significance as well. Attachment to ingroups and preferences of ingroups over outgroups may be universal characteristics of human social life."). See also, D.M. Mackie & J. Cooper, "Attitude Polarization: Effects of Group Membership," 46 *J. Personality & Soc. Psychol.* 575–85 (1984) (indicating that individuals are more likely to change their opinions when confronted with the differing opinions of ingroup members than outgroup members); J.C. Turner et al., "Referent Informational Influence and Group Polarization," 28 *Brit. J. Soc. Psychol.* 135–47 (1989) (same).

27. This type of role-modeling benefit is often assumed in the press but has not been well tested. See Tim Paluch, "WNBA Putting Wrong Butts in Seats," *Iowa St. Daily,* July 26, 2001, available at 2001 WL 24682513 (describing the WNBA as "a feminist sports league showcasing strong-willed female athletes in a male-dominated business. Young girls aspire to be like these women...."); Jeff Passan, "Here's a Good Way to Make a Father's Day—Dads are Taking Their Daughters to the Liberty," *Star-Ledger* (Newark, N.J.), June 17, 2001, available at 2001 WL 22439688. The article quotes a parenting expert as saying that the WNBA players are good role models for girls because they give girls the message that "[y]ou can be out there. You can be out there in the forefront. It is not just boys who play

sports. It forces the idea that women can play sports and can play them well." See also Paul Farhi, "They Got Game, But Few Fans; Women's Teams Struggle to Increase Audiences," *Wash Post,* June 7, 2001, at A1, available at 2001 WL 17634011, (quoting the founding editor of *Sports Illustrated for Women* as saying: "Our research showed there is this tremendous hunger among high school and college-aged girls for role models. They want to see people who look like them doing sports.").

28. Moreover, proportionality may be a particularly appealing way to operationalize the role-modeling effect because it fits well within one of our most basic models for distributing educational resources among social groups: a pre-*Brown* separate but equal model. Of course, the fact that proportionality may look like some version of separate but equal provides no independent justification for the policy. Separate but equal must itself be grounded on some theoretical principle regarding the fair distribution of social rewards.

29. Andrew Koppelman makes a similar cultural transformation argument when discussing the purpose of race-based antidiscrimination law. He argues that the purpose and goal of antidiscrimination law is to reconstruct the social reality and social meanings that define particular social groups as inferior. See Andrew Koppelman, *Antidiscrimination Law & Social Equality* 93–101 (1996).

30. See *supra* note 16.

8

A Comment on the Report of the Commission to Review Title IX Enforcement in Athletics

Earl C. Dudley, Jr. and George Rutherglen

The report of the Commission appointed by the Secretary of Education to study the future of Title IX tries, quite understandably, to walk a middle path. It recognizes the enormous contribution that Title IX—and Title IX enforcement modes—have made to the growth of women's sports and, hence, to the physical and psychological well-being of women in our society. It urges continued vigorous implementation of the statutory mandate of nondiscrimination. At the same time, it acknowledges that progress in women's sports has, to some degree, come at the price of support for men's "minor," "non-revenue," or—in the terminology in vogue today—"Olympic" sports. And it encourages regulators, educators, and athletics administrators to seek new ways to measure compliance with the legislative directive.

We have argued in another place that the exclusive emphasis of the Office for Civil Rights on parity between the ratio of men and women in a school's population and the gender breakdown of participation opportunities in intercollegiate athletics is flawed.[1] In our view, it fails to define the market properly because it takes no account of the relative athletic interests and strengths of the students in a given population, and it ignores the statute's explicit ban on the use of exclusive statistical measures. So we find little that is in the report with which to disagree.

Where the report comes up short is in its failure to tackle head-on the basic resource allocation dilemma of college sports. Succinctly stated, the dilemma is that overall revenues for college athletics are leveling off, if not falling, while expenditures for existing programs are rising. It will not be possible—in the near term, at least—to continue to expand participation opportunities for women by adding new sports without corresponding cuts in men's sports. There are only so many dollars to go around, and at many if not most schools today, every dollar added to women's programs must come from a corresponding reduction in expenditures for existing men's programs. The problem is most severe at state institutions, the majority of which operate under laws requiring that athletic programs be economically self-sustaining. Private colleges and universities, which are not so constrained, may choose to allocate as many resources to athletics as they deem advisable.

Today, most public Division I athletics programs are suffering significant economic strains. Television, the cash cow that has sustained major college athletics for decades, shows signs of weariness. The airwaves are simply clogged with football and basketball broadcasting, and there is little prospect that revenues will continue to grow at the spectacular rate that has marked the last several decades. Football, by far the largest revenue producer among college sports, is struggling to hold its own, yet it remains the centerpiece of funding for most athletic programs. Hence, it is not only untouchable in terms of emphasis and money, but its expenditure needs constantly expand through what the Commission rightly calls the "arms race" of ever spiffier facilities and ever higher coaches' salaries.

For a number of years, while television and gate revenues for football and basketball were rising dramatically, it was possible for many schools to embark on Title IX compliance programs by simply adding women's sports. Those days are gone for now, if not forever. Absent unusual circumstances, a school trying to move toward compliance with the enrollment parity standard must contemplate cuts in emphasis, and perhaps even participation opportunities, for men's sports. This has been happening for years. The hardest hit have been men's gymnastics, which no longer has enough programs to qualify for holding a national championship under NCAA rules, and wrestling.

It is not easy to make the resource allocation decisions facing most collegiate athletic programs, and what to do about football—the largest squad in all collegiate sports—lies at the center of the regulatory aspect of the dilemma. NCAA rules permit Division I schools to offer up to eighty-five full scholarships or their equivalents for football, but there is no corresponding sport for women—as is the case with basketball, soccer, lacrosse, and others—and there is no women's sport with a squad nearly that large. Some have argued that because it is in some ways *sui generis* and because it produces so much revenue, football should not be counted in the effort to measure Title IX compliance. The problems with that approach are obvious. It would insulate the largest and most powerful sport—and its eighty-five-plus participation opportunities—from the mandate of non-discrimination. Thus, it would skew any measure of compliance to the clear detriment of women. On the other hand, inclusion of football in the mix creates almost as many headaches. It means that Division I men's sports other than football must collectively suffer a deficit of eighty-five-plus participation opportunities and scholarships *vis-a-vis* women's sports. The upshot is that a school will often create only a women's team in a dual gender sport, such as tennis, swimming, or crew, or worse, will cut an established men's team in such a sport while creating or maintaining a women's team in the same sport, which is hardly an edifying spectacle in the name of ending gender discrimination in sports.

The problem extends beyond participation opportunities, regardless of how nondiscrimination in such opportunities is to be measured. Because of the perceived economic importance of football, it is a given that most schools will support it to the upper limit of NCAA allowance. That means that, even if participation opportunities have been allocated by a school in a non-discriminatory manner, men's sports other than football start with a deficit of up to eighty-five scholarships as compared to women's sports. It follows that the women's teams will be able to recruit a larger group of more talented athletes, while the men's teams suffer in foreordained mediocrity.

Supporters of some men's "Olympic" sports have sought to solve the problem by endowing scholarships and funds for other expenditures for their individual sports, thus seeking to force the college or university to find some solution other than cutting or reducing support for men's teams. But all this accomplishes in today's regulatory environment is to tie the hands of university administrators who need all the flexibility they can get to deal with an enormous economic and regulatory mess. By committing the school to expend a certain amount on, for example, the men's baseball team, supporters of that sport force it to spend an equivalent (or proportionally equivalent) amount on women's sports, when the soundest economic solution may be to reduce the school's sports menu on some gender-equitable basis.

We can explore the dimensions of the resource allocation dilemma through a hypothetical case involving a fairly typical university. Assume a medium-to-large- sized state university with a long history of supporting a broad menu of sports for both men and women—say, a dozen sports for each gender. Assume further that the university aspires to be a major national player in intercollegiate athletics and that it gauges its success by its ranking in the annual Sears Cup competition, where it hopes to rank in the top ten to fifteen schools each year. Assume further that the university has strong programs in football and men's and women's basketball, the only sports that bring in any revenue, and that it believes that the success of these programs is the most important factor in achieving national visibility and enhancing both the resources available for other sports and the loyalty and generosity of its alumni. Assume also that the university's undergraduate student population is evenly divided between men and women and that the university has achieved parity between its enrollment ratio and its participation opportunities: half of its student athletes are women and half are men.[2] Finally, assume that the university plans to award 300 athletic scholarships or full-time equivalents (FTEs).

The first thing to note about this hypothetical is that Title IX commands, with no available exceptions, that the 300 scholarships be divided equally between men and women. It is important to emphasize that this is true regardless of the source of funding for the scholarships. Thus, if the baseball team raises money on its own for scholarships earmarked specifically for baseball, those scholarships still count toward the men's total and must be offset by the award of a similar number of scholarships to women. Therefore, our hypothetical men's program must get 150 scholarships or FTEs overall, and the women's program must get the same number. Given the commitment to football and men's and women's basketball, those sports will be given the maximum number of scholarships allowed by the NCAA. For football, the number permitted is eighty-five, for men's basketball the number is fourteen, and for women's basketball it is thirteen. Thus, on the men's side, roughly two-thirds—99 out of 150—of the scholarships are taken up by these two sports, leaving fifty-one scholarships available for the ten remaining. By contrast, on the women's side after basketball, there are 137 scholarships to distribute among eleven sports. On a per-sport basis, then, men's "Olympic" sports average 5.1 scholarships apiece, while women's sports other than basketball average 12.45 scholarships each. There is no escaping this calculation, given the requirements of Title IX and the inclusion of football in the mix.

It is obvious what this means for both the men's and women's programs in the aggregate. Since there is no women's sport with a squad size anywhere near that of football, an award of 12.45 scholarships would make almost any women's team highly competitive, and not merely in any existing conference, but nationally as well. On the men's side, however, spreading the pain equally—giving each sport 5.1 scholarship FTEs—would doom all the teams (with the possible exception of golf) to unrelieved, if somewhat respectable, mediocrity.

There are, of course, many ways to spread the available scholarships among the men's non-revenue sports, although a number of considerations impinge upon the choice. To begin, the widespread mediocrity that would ensue from an equal division of the scholarships would almost certainly mean that no men's sport other than football and basketball could regularly earn Sears Cup points. The other most obvious method of distributing the scholarships is to preserve the ability of certain traditionally strong sports to compete at a high level and hence earn Sears Cup points, while lowering the level of support to less successful programs. Given the desire to compete for the rewards of visibility represented by success in the Sears Cup, our hypothetical university is driven to severe "tiering" of its support for men's non-revenue sports.

Some schools avoid this dilemma by offering very restricted varsity menus and fully supporting all their sports. A school with a 50/50 gender breakdown could, for example, give the maximum number of scholarships in football and men's basketball, plus one or two other sports, and then fund a slightly larger number of women's sports, up to the number of scholarships awarded to men. That has not been the path chosen by most colleges and universities, and it would be unfortunate if the soundest way to comply with a statute designed to increase opportunities would be to constrict them severely.

The discussion of our hypothetical has proceeded up to this point as if money were no consideration. That is clearly not the case, however, at most schools. As noted above, projected revenues overall are not likely to keep pace with increasing costs in the foreseeable future, and many athletics departments have been losing money and eating into previously accumulated financial reserves for several years. Absent a major infusion of new resources, our hypothetical university cannot continue its current level of support for intercollegiate athletics, let alone fund a significant increase in women's sports to address the growing proportion of women in undergraduate programs. Moreover, there is a limit to the amount of athletic success that even a very wealthy university can afford. The difficulty is not so much in raising money for athletic scholarships. Instead, the problem is that success has a price tag far beyond the number of scholarships that must be funded. The most immediate and obvious cost of success in a sport is increased travel expenses. To compete at a national level, a team must schedule nonconference games against outstanding teams all across the country. Coaches capable of taking their teams to higher levels command higher salaries. Then there is the issue of facilities. The well-funded programs that compete at the national level in all the nonrevenue sports tend to have attractive, up-to-date facilities, which swiftly become a major factor in recruiting the best athletes coming out of high school.

In summation, something has to give. The difficulty is that as a practical matter it almost certainly won't be football. That means that men's and women's non-revenue sports must find a *modus vivendi* that will allow continued expansion of opportunities for women and support for women's programs without gradually killing off traditional—and valuable—sports programs for men. While we do not know what that *modus vivendi* should look like, we remain of the view that the enrollment parity standard of the Office for Civil Rights is more of a hindrance than a help, especially given the emerging demographics of college attendance. As experience under other cognate constitutional and statutory norms demonstrates, there are many possible approaches to defining "discrimination" under Title IX. Flexibility and the willingness to compromise will be needed to resolve the current and future dilemma, as they always are when more than one group has legitimate claims to a finite cluster of resources that is not large enough to satisfy all claimants. Those qualities may be in short supply in today's politicized and polarized environment, but there ought to be common ground on which progress can be made. There are, for example, some obvious economies of scale in dual gender sports, where performance and training facilities—and sometimes coaches and equipment—can be shared. For these and other reasons, the regulatory scheme should encourage schools to field both men's and women's teams in dual gender sports, and not cut men's teams to reach some arbitrary statistical definition of parity. Creativity, encouragement, and education should be the watchwords of regulators. Rigid formulas will not solve such a major and complex problem.

Notes

1. See Earl C. Dudley, Jr., and George Rutherglen, Ironies, Inconsistencies, and Intercollegiate Athletics: Title IX, Title VII, and Statistical Evidence of Discrimination, 1 *Va. J. Sports & Law* 177 (1999).
2. Of course, women currently make up somewhere on the order of 57 percent of the undergraduate student population nationwide.

9

How to Evaluate the Implementation of Title IX at Colleges and Universities and Attitudes and Interest of Students Regarding Athletics

Barbara Murray

The following was written as an assignment for a Graduate School of Education class, titled Program and Policy Analysis, at the University of Pennsylvania. The students were instructed by Professor Rebecca Maynard to develop a research plan for a topic of interest to them. "How to Evaluate the Implementation of Title IX at Colleges and Universities and Attitudes and Interest of Students Regarding Athletics" was selected by Barbara Murray.

Upon approaching the thirtieth anniversary, women athletes have been poised to support their position on Title IX, the federal regulations established in 1972 to ensure gender equity in college and university sports. Adding to the list of heavyweights—no athletic reference intended—was actress Geena Davis, an amateur archer, who joined the ranks of women athletes rallying outside the final public forum held by the Commission on Opportunity in Athletics. Among other information, statistics that showed few girls were interested in playing sports went challenged by Ms. Davis, who claimed these statistics were skewed, and weakening Title IX, based on such numbers, was "unfair." She exclaimed, "I am here to take you for a short ride in Thelma and Louise's car if you think it's fair and just to limit a girl's opportunity to play sports based on her response to an interest survey" (*The Daily Times*, 2002).

What Is Title IX?

Title IX, of the Education Amendments of 1972, is a federal law that was enacted to bar sex discrimination in all facets of education, including sports programs. Title IX prohibits any federally funded education program or activity from engaging in sex discrimination (National Coalition for Women and Girls in Education, 2002). It states:

No person in the United States shall, on the basis of sex, be excluded from participation in, be denied the benefit of or be subjected to discrimination under any education program or activity receiving Federal financial assistance. (20 U.S.C. Section 1681)

In fact, Title IX itself was slipped into a civil-rights law because conservative Southerners thought the idea of granting equal opportunities for women would derail the bill. Thirty years after its passage it's still the most controversial topic in college sports (Suggs, 2002a).

In order to be in compliance with Title IX and its application to athletics, a school need only comply with one of the following so-called "three prong" tests:

1. Commonly called "proportionality," the number of athletes from each sex should be roughly equivalent to the enrollment percentages. In other words, if women make up half the student population, about half the athletes should be women.
2. A school should show a history and continuing practice of adding women's sports.
3. A school should be able to show the athletic interests and abilities of women are being fully and effectively accommodated.

Under [these] regulations, a school can demonstrate compliance by showing it meets one of the three standards. Colleges and universities, on advice of counsel, have generally tried to meet the first standard, [that of] proportionality. In doing so, this has led them to add sports for women and eliminate non-revenue-producing sports for men, some athletic directors contend. Roughly 55 percent of the nation's undergraduates are female.

Some proponents of women's athletics fear that the commission would attempt to make it easier for institutions to move away from proportionality and to rely instead on the third prong—in which they can use surveys of the student body to determine what they have to provide (Eichel, 2002).

Interpretation and Enforcement of Title IX

The Federal Government is responsible for enforcing Title IX. The Department of Education's Office for Civil Rights (ORC) is the "primary agency charged with making Title IX's mandate a reality. OCR has the power to withhold federal funding from a school that refuses to comply with the law, although OCR has never used this powerful tool." In its 1996 clarification, the OCR called the proportionality test a "safe harbor." Some athletic directors have come to think of it as the safest way to pass. Attorney Larry Joseph, who represents the coalition of coaches challenging the regulations, says many athletic directors worry about the second and third parts as they are difficult to quantify: "How do you fully accommodate if you can't be sure what 'fully' means?" (Brady, 2002a)

As many schools use "proportionality" to comply with Title IX, there are many critics who regard this as simply filling quotas. In doing so, Stephen P. Erber, Director of Athletics at Muhlenberg College in Allentown, PA, writes the "The current interpretation of Title IX, which allows institutions to come into compliance by achieving a certain gender ratio (or quota) is exactly what enables those same institutions to avoid redistributing existing resources in order to enhance women's athletics programs" (Letters to the Editor, 2000). He sights the original legislation by saying that it, in fact, precludes ratios and quotas, stating that

> nothing shall be interpreted to require any educational institution to grant preferential or disparate treatment to the members of one sex on account of an imbalance which may exist with respect to the total number or percentage of persons of that sex participating in or receiving the benefits of any federally supported program or activity, in comparison with the total number of percentage of persons of that sex in any community. (20 U.S.C. Sec. 1681 (b))

Erber also suggests that groups such as The Center for Individual Rights and the Independent Women's Forum are asking for the elimination of the proportionality test, the use of the other two tests (accommodating interests and a history of expansion) as the only mea-

TABLE 1
Title IX Timeline

June 23, 1972	Title IX bans sex discrimination in schools.
1974	U.S. Senate passes, but House fails to pass, an amendment that would exclude revenue-producing sports from Title IX.
1978	Health, Education and Welfare Department provides final guidelines for schools.
1979	The Northwest Women's Law Center is successful in a lawsuit against Washington State University, forcing the school to comply with Title IX.
1984	In *Grove City College vs. Bell*, the Supreme Court rules that only programs that receive federal funding and not the entire college fall under Title IX.
1988	Civil Right Restoration Act overturns the *Grove City* decision, saying that Title IX applies to all operations of a college receiving federal funds.
1997	Supreme Court upholds a lower court ruling that found Brown University in violation of Title IX. The suit that forced the ruling, *Cohen vs. Brown University*, came when Brown dropped women's gymnastics.
1997	Stephen Neal, the 1996 NCAA heavyweight wrestling champion from Cal State-Bakersfield, sues the university for trying to eliminate wrestling to comply with Title IX. A federal judge blocks the school from disbanding wrestling; the case is pending.
1998	U.S. District Court Judge Ernest Torres approves Brown University's plan for complying with Title IX, the final issue in the lawsuit that has become the standard for compliance. The university agrees to keep the percentage of female athletes within 3.5 percent of Brown's female student population.
2001	As a result of Title IX, enrollment of women in athletics programs and professional schools has increased dramatically. For example, before Title IX, 7.4 percent of high school athletes in the U.S. were female. In 2001, the number rose to 41.5 percent.
January 16, 2002	A federal lawsuit brought by the National Wrestling Coaches Association seeks to protect sports from being eliminated from schools for the purpose of complying with Title IX.
August 27–28, 2002	The first of (five) public forums on Title IX is held in Atlanta. On the 30th anniversary of Title IX, the Secretary of Education requested the forums and asks Women's Sports Foundation to report back its findings by January 2003.

Source: Post-Gazette.com. Lifestyle, *Title IX Timeline*. October 6, 2002.

sure of Title IX compliance, and a return to the original intent of Title IX so that colleges and universities actually enhance and expand women's athletic opportunities, rather than reducing or eliminating men's athletic opportunities (Letters to the Editor, 2000).

It should be clear that Title IX doesn't require identical athletic programs for males and females. Under Title IX, one team is not compared to the same team in each sport, and therefore does not require that each team receive exactly the same services and supplies. Rather, Title IX requires that the men's and women's programs receive a similar or comparable level of service, facilities, supplies, etc. Variations within the men's and women's programs are allowed, as long as they are justified on a nondiscriminatory basis (U.S. Department of Education, 2002).

Athletics before Title IX

Prior to 1972, women and girls looking for opportunities for athletic competition were more likely to try out for cheerleading or secure places in the bleachers as spectators. In 1971, fewer than 30,000 females competed in intercollegiate athletics. Low participation rates reflected the lack of institutional commitment to providing athletics programming for women. Before Title IX, female college athletes received only 2 percent of overall athletic budgets, and athletic scholarships for women were virtually nonexistent. As one of my colleagues commented over a lunch meeting on the topic of Title IX, men were expected to engage in sporting activities throughout their entire youth. It was a rite of passage, if you will. For men, one of the most often asked question was "In what sports will you be participating?", whereas women were never asked, nor expected to address, this question. They were often invited to take home economics or library studies, but never expected to join in an athletic activity. It seemed to have more to do with fragility, however, versus a downright exclusion from participation.

Rulings Regarding Title IX

Table 1 presents some of the key rulings regarding Title IX. It is important to note that although the rulings have largely been in favor of Title IX and thus women in sports, no school has had federal funds withdrawn as a result of the decision.

One problem with bringing Title IX complaints against colleges is not knowing how much money a college or university is putting into women's and men's sports. Thanks to a 1994 amendment, which went into effect in 1996, colleges and universities are now required to disclose funding and participation rates. Students and prospective students can now ask a university's athletics department for a report on expenditures and participation rates broken down by gender (Feminist Majority Foundation, 1995).

Commission on Athletic Opportunity

A fifteen-member commission was formed, appointed by the Bush Administration to address the issue of equity in athletic opportunities of both men and women. The members include representatives of academic, athletic, government, and research communities, in addition to other persons with special expertise in intercollegiate and secondary school athletics or issues of equal educational opportunity (U.S. Department of Education, 2002). The Commission was charged with reviewing Title IX's standards for assessing equal opportunity in athletics. In addition, the Commission's goal is to examine ways to strengthen enforcement and expand opportunities to ensure fairness for all college athletes. Five public forums across the country were held to gather the facts and listen to what the American people had to say, and discover how Title IX was serving our citizens (Cooper, 2002).

Their focus was to address seven questions. The questions to be answered were as follows:

- Are Title IX standards for assessing equal opportunity in athletics working to promote opportunities for male and female athletics?
- Is there adequate Title IX guidance that enables colleges and school districts to know what is expected of them and to plan for an athletic program that effectively meets the needs and interests of their students?
- Is further guidance or other steps needed in junior or senior high levels where the availability or absence of opportunities will critically affect the prospective interests and abilities of student athletics when they do reach college age?
- How should activities such as cheerleading and bowling factor into the analysis of equitable opportunities?
- How do revenue producing and large-roster teams affect equal opportunity in athletics?

- In what ways do opportunities and other sports venues, such as Olympics, professional leagues and community recreation programs, interact with the obligations of colleges and school districts to provide equal opportunity in athletics?
- Apart from Title IX enforcement, are there other efforts to promote athletic opportunities for male and female students that the department might support, such as public-private partnerships to support the efforts of schools and colleges in this area?

Sentiments of Colleges and Universities

Marcia Greenberger, co-president of the National Women's Law Center, feels the question to be asked by the commission is: "What else needs to be done for women?" The impetus behind forming the commission appears to rest on an opposite question: Is the implementation of Title IX at some colleges unfair to men? Maryland athletics director Deborah Yow, one of the commission members, remarked, "I understand that some people think we should not be looking at this issue, but I applaud the fact we are getting the chance. Thirty years later, it's not unusual to want to assess where we are. Title IX is a great law and I have benefited from it immensely, but it's a good time to take a step back and look at the big picture. There is always room for improvement" (Brady, 2002b).

Opinions regarding Title IX legislation run the spectrum from qualified satisfaction to guarded frustration. Among women, it is widely felt they still have a long road to travel before they attain equity in college sports. Female athletes still play in inferior facilities, stay in lower-caliber hotels on the road, eat in cheaper restaurants, benefit from smaller promotional budgets, and have fewer assistant coaches (*The Chronicle Review*, 2000).

The critics of Title IX argue that the "substantial proportionality, the first option, essentially establishes an absolute limit on the number of male athletes in an athletics department" (Mr. LeSher, president of Iowans Against Quotas). He also suggests, as do others, that because more men than women typically go out for sports, [the proportionality] test discriminates against men" (Suggs, 2000). On the other hand, "Athletic directors just want to keep lawyers and civil-rights investigators out of their offices" (Suggs, 2002a).

Prior Research

Prior research, particularly since 1996, has focused on numbers: how many students enrolled, by gender; how many students are participating in athletics, by gender; and budgetary spending, by gender. To date, little has been done in the area of what feelings and motivations make women choose to participate or not participate in sports. Statistical data has revealed that both men's and women's participation has increased during the past thirty years, but the indicators for what has specifically brought about these changes is lacking. One study was performed by Baker, Heinrich, and Miller in 2000, in which they surveyed a Division II university. Their study was designed to:

1. Determine female students' interest in sports;
2. Determine whether students think their university is in compliance with Title IX; and
3. Compare the interests in sports exhibited by male and female students.

In the first part of the study, female students' interest in sports was compared to opportunities offered by the university. The subjects were randomly selected and then contacted by phone; in all, 382 women completed the "Student Interest in Athletics, Sports, and Physical Fitness Survey" (NCAA, 1995). Most of the surveyed women (92 percent) were Caucasian. Results revealed that time-related constraints, not interest, were the primary reasons why some women chose not to participate in college athletics. The respondents also reported that they were generally satisfied with the athletic programs offered, which suggests that the university was in compliance with Title IX. In the second part of the study, the interest level of female respondents was compared to that of male respondents. Most of the 108 students (forty-six males, sixty-two females) who were surveyed were Caucasian. The same NCAA questionnaire was used. Males reported higher interest in athletics, fitness, and sports activities than females. Male students also had a much higher participation level in high school varsity sports than women. However, women had a greater desire to participate in sports in which they were not currently participating (Back, 2001).

Conclusions of Prior Research

In general, it is impossible to tell whether a particular institution is in compliance with Title IX just by examining reports, according to Mary Frances O'Shea, coordinator of Title IX issues in sports for the U.S. Department of Education's Office of Civil Rights. However, the reports do show, informally, that women appear to be making substantial gains on the playing fields and locker rooms of Division I. (*More Women Participate in Intercollegiate Athletics*, Athletics, *The Chronicle of Higher Education*, May 21, 1999)

A disadvantage of telephone surveys, as mentioned above, is that those with unlisted numbers are automatically excluded from the survey, which may bias the results. In addition, most people are bombarded with junk phone calls, so when an interviewer calls they may think it's just another telemarketer and hang up. People also tend to disregard unfamiliar numbers when they have call identification (Ary et al., 2002).

Past research has also indicated that women, as well as all participants, have benefited from participation in sports. For example,

- Competitive athletics promotes responsible social behaviors, greater successes, and increase personal skills (Carnegie Corporation, 1996, as reported in the National Women's Law Center, 2002).
- Adolescent female athletes have lower rates of both sexual activity and pregnancy (Women's Sports Foundation Report: Sport and Teen Pregnancy, 1998 and The President's Council on Physical Fitness and Sports Report, *Physical Activity & Sports in the Lives of Girls*, 1997).

Proposal Overview

This study is designed to support one of the recommendations submitted to the Department of Education's Secretary, Rod Paige, by the Commission on Athletic Opportunity. Recommendation 18 states the following:

The Office for Civil Rights should allow institutions to conduct continuous interest surveys on a regular basis as a way of (1) demonstrating compliance with the three-part test, (2) allowing schools to accurately predict and reflect men's and women's interest in athletics over time, and (3) stimulating student interest in varsity sports. The Office should specify the criteria necessary for conducting such a survey in a way that is clear and understandable.

Table 2

Logic Model for Evaluating the Attitudes and Interests of Students in Conjunction with Effectiveness of Title IX

Antecedents	Implementation	Intermediate Effects	Outcomes
Student Characteristics	**Students**	**Students**	**Students**
o Age	o Recruitment of men/women	o Greater self-esteem in all participating in sports	o Implementation of Title IX demonstrably impacting women's participation in sports
o M or F	o Athletic opportunities desired	o Less likelihood to become involved in less than desirable activities	o Rewarding college experience through participation in athletics
o High school attended	o Athletic opportunities enrolled	o Greater commitment to school and school spirit	
o Sports experience in high school and prior			**School**
Parents History	**Schools**	**Parents**	o Ability to assess students' abilities and interest in athletics
o Marital status	o Athletic opportunities made available	o More involvement with their child	o Ability to use data to determine which sporting programs to initiate or eliminate
o Parent(s) working	o Athletic opportunities promoted	o More interaction with school activities	o Ability to defend decisions made
o Income		o More awareness of the policies governing school, particularly athletic issues	o Ability to remain in compliance with Title IX more accurately and effectively
o Attend college			o Bank of 'best practices'
o Sports experience		**Schools**	
o Student enrollment		o Improve relationships overall regarding Title IX legislation	
School		o Understanding	
o Total enrollment by men/women		o Implementation	
o Participation in sports by men/women			
o Athletic budget by men/women			
o Athletic salaries by men/women			

The study's goal is to assist the Commission in the above efforts, as well as determine what motivates both men and women in their pursuit of athletic endeavors. In this study a "pilot" would be employed to evaluate the implementation of Title IX and review the patterns and preparedness of the men and women regarding their participation in sports by sampling a small number of colleges and universities. The hope is that by gathering this information on behalf of colleges and universities, these institutions will have a mechanism to more readily conform to more than one prong of the three-pronged test outlined in Title IX's regulations.

Upon selecting five pilot colleges and universities to participate in this evaluation, the first goal will be to ascertain whether or not the school understands the implications of Title IX and whether, in fact, there are policies in place which have been communicated throughout the educational community. In addition, the focus would concentrate on what motivates women and men to participate in sports at the college and university level and has the understanding and implementation of Title IX assisted in that goal. The study will also attempt to correlate universities who have not instituted any additional effort to comply with Title IX versus ones who have significantly altered their athletic programs in the wake of the 1972 ruling, and its impact, or lack thereof, of participation by men and women in sports. In providing the Commission with this information, this may be a first step towards exploring their recommendations.

Table 2 shows a proposed logic model that outlines the antecedents, implementation, intermediate effects, and outcomes to be realized.

Study Design

To begin, the study proposes a pilot using a representative sample of institutions with established athletic programs for both men and women. It should be noted that while it may be difficult to include a college or university which *has not* incorporated any enhancements to their athletic programs since Title IX was instituted, we felt it was worth attempting this at the outset. By including this information a bank of data will be collected that consists of "best practices" of these colleges and universities. The goal will be to determine if colleges and universities did or did not employ extraordinary measure to comply with Title IX, and whether or not this affected the "attitudes and interests" of their students. The overarching research question we are proposing is to see, as stated by Professor Rebecca Maynard, Program Policy and Analysis, University of Pennsylvania, "What are the factors that determine why men and women participate in sports and how they relate to the operational actions that were taken in response to Title IX."

From the College or University

The major research questions we would initially seek to determine from colleges and universities are as follows:

- What has the impact of Title IX been on the university?
- What are the policies for the enforcement of Title IX?
- What is the proportion of male and female students to the male and female athletes?
- What are the opportunities available to men and women and how are these opportunities made available, advertised?

From the Students

Freshmen
- What were your athletic interests and opportunities in high school?
- What are your athletic interests in college?

Seniors
- Were athletic opportunities available to you, in which you were interested?
- In what athletic opportunities did you participate?

Project Plan

Phase I

Our first step will be to send out "Requests for Participation" inviting colleges and universities to participate in what will, as mentioned, initially be a pilot study.

An outline of the benefits to the prospective college or university should be included in our initial letter to encourage their participation. Much of the information we will be seeking from their administrative areas is currently required of them and should be readily available, thus lessening the burden of work on the part of the college or university. In the proposal, the new information to be obtained will largely be supplied by the students in what would be considered a rather low maintenance approach, simultaneously seeking to gather other pertinent information of interest for supplemental areas of the college and university. Upon positive replies from a college and/or university disposed to participate in the pilot and the selection of five sample colleges, we will categorize them according to the following:

- Enrollment by men and women
- Budget
- Size/location
- Primary area of study
- Athletic opportunities available

From here, we will begin to arrange meetings with each institution and via executive interviews, ask a series of questions to determine their understanding of Title IX and the implementation process employed. The impact of this review will establish the basis of the study and will be used in conjunction with the data gathered from the students.

Phase II

Employing a longitudinal "cohort" study, the participating college or university in the study will be asked to survey their incoming freshmen as well as their outgoing seniors on an annual basis to determine the attitudes and trends in the desires of their students. In this study, we will follow a specific population, the freshman upon entering college, and follow-up, in this case, when they are seniors. In this way, we'll be able to assess if their attitudes and interests have changed over time as they become more exposed to and familiar with the opportunities available to them.

The plan proposes surveying the students with directly administered questionnaires that will incorporate a variety of information important to all administrative functions, such as dining, shopping, social, fraternities/sororities, and other similar extracurricular activities. In framing the questionnaires in this fashion, we will avoid any threats to internal validity, particularly the Hawthorne effect, where there is a tendency for a subject to change their behavior just because they are participating in an experiment—in this case, a survey (Ary et al., 2002). In addition, this approach will garner more information useful to the college and the university and, in the long run, the students as well.

We are suggesting that the questionnaires be administered during an assembly or meeting of all college freshmen upon their arrival to the school. The same format would be followed when these students become seniors. We recommend this idea versus mailing questionnaires to the students as the response rate will, without question, be significantly greater.

Proposed Outcomes

Pending the results of the pilot study, we may want to propose the Commission on Athletic Opportunity adopt surveying the administration, along with the student body, as a future mandatory requirement of all schools. This may give credence to the application of Title IX, and also assist colleges and universities in defending their position as to why certain decisions are made with regard to athletic programs initiated or eliminated.

One of the main issues that has been raised by critics of Title IX is that the majority of colleges and universities use the first of the three prong test, proportionality in enrollment, in their efforts to comply. In doing so, the reasons for the elimination of men's sports have been directly related to this factor. With the inclusion of a student survey, colleges and universities will be able to point to other factors that may lead to the retention, removal, or explanation of why certain sports are predominantly, or equally, available for women or men. This approach, versus the enrollment of men and women, would seem to be a more equitable distribution for directing athletic opportunities and resources.

In addition, the students would benefit by such implementations that might not otherwise be available to them based on enrollments alone. The turnaround for students' ideas might not be readily seen by the initial respondents of the surveys, but over time the trends of students' attitudes and interests would become more evident.

As this is only a pilot study to determine if, in fact, there is a relationship between whether or not the attitudes and interests might be attributed to the efforts towards implementing Title IX regulations, or the lack thereof, the Commission may decide to use the information to recommend, or perhaps mandate, that other schools follow a similar plan of action, such as surveying the student body.

References

Ary et al. 2002. *Introduction to Research in Education.*

Brady, Erich. 2002a. Time Fails to Lessen Title IX Furor. *USA Today*, 19 June.

Brady, Erich. 2002b. Panel Eager to Assess 'Where We Are'. *USA Today*, 30 June.

Carnegie Corporation. 1996. *The Role of Sports in Youth Development*, March, as reported in the National Women's Law Center, May 2002.

The Chronicle of Higher Education. 1999. More Women Participate in Intercollegiate Athletics, 21 May.

The Chronicle Review. 2000. Backlash Against Title IX: An End Run Around Female Athletes, 3 March.

Cooper, Cynthia. 2002. Chicago Town Hall Meeting, The Drake Hotel, September 17. *The Daily Times.* 2002. Wire Reports. 22 November.

Eichel, Larry. 2002. Title IX Advisory Commission Meets in Philadelphia. *The Philadelphia Inquirer*, 6 December.

Feminist Majority Foundation. 1995. *Empowering Women in Sports.*

Letters to the Editor. 2000. *The Chronicle of Higher Education*, 31 March.

National Coalition for Women and Girls in Education. 2002. Title IX Athletics Policies: Issues and Data for Educational Decision Makers, August 27.

Post-gazette.com. 2002. *Lifestyle, Title IX Timeline.* 6 October

The President's Council on Physical Fitness and Sports. 1997. *Physical Activity & Sports in the Lives of Girls.*

Suggs, Welch. 2000. Foes of Title IX Try to Make Equity in College Sports a Campaign Issue. *The Chronicle of Higher Education*, 4 February.

Suggs, Welch. 2002a. Title IX at 30. *The Chronicle of Higher Education*, 21 June.

Suggs, Welch. 2002b. Federal Commission Considers Reinterpreting Title IX. *The Chronicle of Higher Education*, September 6.

U.S. Department of Education. 2002. Q & A—Secretary's Commission on Opportunity in Athletics, August 19.

Women's Sports Foundation Report. 1998. Sport and Teen Pregnancy, 1998

10

Lessons from Research on Title IX and Intercollegiate Athletics

John J. Cheslock and Deborah J. Anderson

In 2003, the Commission on Opportunities in Athletics revisited the application of Title IX to intercollegiate athletics. In this chapter, we first review the existing social science research on topics integral to the debate undertaken by the Commission, focusing especially on our own findings for the period 1995/96 to 2001/02 (Anderson and Cheslock, 2004; Anderson, Cheslock, and Ehrenberg, 2004; Cheslock and Anderson, 2004). Then, we discuss implications of this research for the debate over Title IX and the current manner in which it is enforced. We do not tackle the question of whether or not substantial proportionality (defined below) is the best or even an appropriate method to measure compliance with Title IX. Rather, we discuss how empirical research can inform the debate over Title IX given the current policy environment that focuses on substantial proportionality.

Overview of Research Findings

Thanks to the passage of the Equity in Athletics Disclosure Act (EADA) in 1994, which requires institutions to provide information on their athletic programs beginning in 1995/96, academic researchers are developing a body of research that investigates some of the key issues relating to Title IX in intercollegiate athletics. This section highlights and discusses the most important findings in this line of research to date.

Finding #1: There is widespread non-compliance with the substantial proportionality prong of Title IX, with some improvement in compliance over time.

With respect to intercollegiate athletics, Title IX applies to three broad areas: financial assistance to athletes; "other program areas" such as "treatment, benefits, and opportunities" for athletes; and "equal opportunity (equally effective accommodation of the interests and abilities of male and female athletes)" (Johnson, 1994, p. 558). It is in reference to the third area that the Office of Civil Rights (OCR) developed the three-prong test that is most commonly associated with Title IX's application to intercollegiate athletics. That is, an institution is in compliance with this portion of Title IX if: the female share of athletes is "substantially proportionate" to the female share of undergraduates; an institution has a "history and continuing practice" of expanding athletic opportunities for women; or the institution is "effectively accommodating the interests and abilities" of prospective female athletes (U.S. Department of Education, 1997, part 5). Although satisfaction of any one of the three prongs signals compliance with Title IX, in recent years compliance had become nearly synonymous with substantial proportionality due to a 1996 OCR policy clarification and several judicial decisions. In July 2003, the OCR released its most recent policy clarification, removing the favored status of the first prong. However, the Department of Education did not provide additional guidance regarding how institutions can comply with the second or third prong; as a result, the courts are unlikely to reduce their reliance on substantial proportionality at this time.

To measure compliance with substantial proportionality, it is common for researchers to calculate a proportionality gap for each institution, as follows:

Proportionality gap = [(% of undergraduates who are female) − (% of athletes who are female)] *100

The OCR has declined to define what gap, if any, would be considered substantially proportionate under Title IX. However, several lawsuit settlements suggest that a gap of 3 percent or 5 percent would be acceptable to a court of law, and as a result, researchers have defined compliance to consist of a differential of no more than three to five percentage points (Anderson, Cheslock, and Ehrenberg, 2004; Farrell, 1995; Sigelman and Wahlbeck, 1999; Stafford, 2004; Zimbalist, 1997).

Using this definition, several researchers have found that a large majority of institutions fail to meet compliance with substantial proportionality (Anderson, Cheslock, and Ehrenberg, 2004; Rishe, 1999; Sigelman and Wahlbeck, 1999; Stafford, 2004; Suggs, 2003). Anderson, Cheslock, and Ehrenberg (2004) find that for their sample of 741 National Collegiate Athletics Association (NCAA) institutions, non-compliance (in terms of women being underrepresented among athletes) decreases from about 90–93 percent of the sample in 1995/96 to about 82–89 percent of the sample in 2001/02, allowing for leeway of 3–5 percentage points in measuring proportionality. Over this same period, the average proportionality gap for all institutions, including those considered compliant, fell from 15.2 to 13.1 percentage points. These results clearly indicate that despite improvements over time, substantial gender inequities in intercollegiate athletic opportunities persist at the vast majority of institutions.

Finding #2: The strategies used to improve compliance vary over time.

Institutions could employ a variety of strategies to improve compliance with the substantial proportionality test. They could "equalize up" by simply increasing the number of female athletes, keeping the number of male athletes the same, to the point of substantial proportionality. Alternatively, they could "equalize down" by decreasing the number of male athletes, while holding the number of female athletes constant, until they reach compliance. Or institutions could use some combination of adding female athletes and dropping male athletes, thereby substituting previous opportunities for men with new opportunities for women. Which strategies should be preferred is a normative question addressed in the next section; here we simply summarize the research that describes the strategies actually used by institutions in their efforts to improve compliance.

One way to roughly measure institutional strategies is to examine how the average number of teams and participants for men and women change over time for a consistent sample of institutions. Two studies provide these estimates for NCAA institutions in different periods:

GAO (1999) focuses on changes between 1985/86 and 1996/97, and Cheslock and Anderson (2004) focus on the 1995/96–2001/02 period. Interestingly, the strategies employed by institutions appear to change over time.

Results from GAO (1999) for the earlier period suggest that, on average, institutions relied on the joint strategy of adding women and decreasing men. For their sample, the total number of teams increased by 17 percent for women and fell by 3 percent for men, while the total number of participants increased by 16 percent for women and fell by 12 percent for men. In contrast, Cheslock and Anderson (2004) find that, on average, institutions primarily used the strategy of equalizing up during the late 1990s. During the six-year period from 1995/96 to 2001/02, the total number of teams increased by 13 percent for women and 1 percent for men; similarly, the number of participants increased by 19 percent for women and only 1 percent for men. One likely explanation for the differences across these periods is that the relative prosperity experienced by institutions of higher education during the late 1990s allowed them to utilize the more expensive strategy of equalizing opportunities through expansion rather than contraction or substitution.

A more direct way to measure institutions' strategies is to examine how decisions to change male and female athletics were influenced by pressures relating to Title IX. For the late 1990s, Anderson and Cheslock (2004) and Cheslock and Anderson (2004) use regression analyses to estimate how institutions that were further from compliance in 1995/ 96 (as measured by the proportionality gap) behaved differently than institutions that were much closer to compliance, all else equal. The results are very similar to the descriptive statistics presented above.

Specifically, we use ordinary least squares regression for four dependent variables: net change in the number of male athletes, female athletes, male teams, and female teams. The explanatory variables include the 1995/96 proportionality gap as well as various institutional characteristics that reflect preferences of institutions and their students, institutions' financial wealth, and structural constraints. Our results show that for men, neither changes in teams nor changes in participants were significantly related to the 1995/96 proportionality gap. In contrast, the proportionality gap had a significant positive effect on changes in both women's teams and participants; further, this relationship was quite substantial in size. Certainly, these results suggest that institutions relied on the strategy of equalizing up during the late 1990s.

Finding #3: Aggregate results for men and women hide considerable differences across sports.

In the popular press, discussions about Title IX often focus on changes in one or a few individual sports. Most notorious are the cases of men's wrestling and gymnastics, which have seen substantial decreases in the number of teams and participants over the 1980s and 1990s. Therefore, it is important to disaggregate the total figures reported above into figures presented separately by sport.

Estimates of changes in teams and participants for individual sports show tremendous differences across sports for each gender, as discussed by GAO (1999) for the period 1985/86 to 1996/97 and Cheslock and Anderson (2004) for the period 1995/96 to 2001/02. For example, some sports like lacrosse and soccer are becoming more popular at the college level and grew substantially over this period for both men and women. The number of lacrosse teams expanded by 19 percent for men and 46 percent for women between 1985/86 and 1996/97. Lacrosse increased even more quickly between 1995/96 and 2001/02, posting gains in teams of 15 percent for men and 48 percent for women. In addition to newly popular sports, some evidence suggests that a few more traditional sports are growing relative to other male sports, although this growth is concentrated in the number of participants rather than the number of teams. For example, between 1995/96 and 2001/02, the average number of football players per institution grew by 6 percent while the average number of baseball players per institution grew by 5 percent. At the same time, the share of institutions offering these sports grew by only 1.7 percent (football) and 0.5 percent (baseball).

Despite these gains for some men's sports, the concern for wrestling and gymnastics is well placed. For men, wrestling teams suffered substantial declines of 30 percent during the earlier period and 13 percent during the later period. Simultaneously, the losses for men's gymnastics were even more alarming: slightly over half of men's gymnastics teams were cut between 1985/86 and 1996/97, and nearly one-third were eliminated between 1995/96 and 2001/02. At the same time, the number of women's gymnastics teams decreased by 36 percent between 1985/86 and 1996/97, and by 5 percent between 1995/96 and 2001/02. Thus, the decline experienced by men's gymnastics, while larger than for women, is not gender specific. Female wrestlers suffered losses as well when the University of Minnesota-Morris announced plans to discontinue the only existing NCAA women's wrestling team after the 2003/04 season.

Finding #4: Aggregate results also hide differences across institutions.

Athletic departments differ in terms of Title IX compliance as well as changes over time in male and female athletics. In this discussion, we focus on differences related to NCAA division as well as other institutional characteristics such as region, selectivity, enrollment, financial wealth, and the like.

NCAA divisions (I, II, and III) differ in several key ways.[1] First, the NCAA requires a minimum number of athletic teams per gender: seven teams in Division I (or, eight teams for women and six teams for men); four teams in Division II; and five teams in Division III. Another major difference is in financial aid awards related to athletic ability. Division I sets both minimum and maximum financial aid award requirements; Division II regulates only maximum financial aid levels; and Division III prohibits financial aid related to students' participation in athletics. A final important dissimilarity is the scale of the athletic programs. For example, Fulks (2002a, 2002b) estimates that athletic expenditures in 2001/02 averaged approximately $23.2 million in Division I-A, $6.7 million in Division I-AA, $5.8 million in Division I-AAA, $2 million in Division II, and $1 million in Division III. Although expenditures in Division I are much higher than in either Division II or III, the most extreme disparity in expenditures exists between Division I-A and all other institutions.

Given these differences, it is not surprising that the trends during the last twenty years contrast sharply across NCAA divisions. With respect to changes over time in the level of compliance with substantial proportionality, Division I institutions improved greatly between 1995/96 and 2001/02, while schools in Division II and III showed very slight progress. For example, the average proportionality gap shrank by almost four points in Division I but fell by only approximately one point in Divisions II and III. As a result, by the end of the period schools in Division I demonstrated much higher compliance rates (17–28 percent) than schools in Divisions II and III (7–12 percent).

One main reason why Division I institutions improved their compliance so significantly between 1995/96 and 2001/02 is that they combined the strategies of equalizing up plus a bit of substitution, while institutions in Divisions II and III relied solely on equalizing up. Specifically, although all divisions increased the number of women athletes on average (by 23 percent in Division I, 24 percent in Division II, and 11 percent in Division III), Division I institutions also reduced the number of men's athletes by 3 percent while Divisions II and III increased male athletes by 5 and 3 percent, respectively (Cheslock and Anderson, 2004). During the earlier period of 1985/86 to 1996/97, differences in trends across division were limited to changes in the number of female athletes. While all divisions decreased male athletes by 10–16 percent, female athletes grew by 29 percent in Division I institutions as compared to only 12 percent in Division III institutions; further, Division II institutions cut female athletes by 2 percent over this period (GAO, 1999).

Finally, it is important to note that athletic division is not the only institutional characteristic that is associated with better or worse levels of compliance. Several authors (Agthe and Billings, 2000; Anderson, Cheslock, and Ehrenberg, 2004; Sigelman and Wahlbeck, 1999; Stafford, 2004) identify other determinants of compliance using a regression framework. For example, institutions located in the Midwest or South and less selective institutions have larger proportionality gaps, all else equal. In contrast, several other factors facilitate compliance. Perhaps most helpful is a relatively small female share of undergraduates, which explains why military academies and schools of technology usually comply at higher rates.[2] In addition, a relatively large student body aids compliance probably because it provides a greater pool of potential female athletes from which to draw. Finally, institutions with more funds, especially due to high tuition and fees, perform better on substantial proportionality, reflecting the necessity of money to field additional women's sports. Interestingly, Stafford (2004) attempts to directly measure the impact of Title IX enforcement on institutional compliance and mostly finds no significant effect of NCAA recertification, complaints filed through the Office of Civil Rights, or Title IX lawsuits.

Finding #5: Football is unlike other college sports and its impact on other sports is unclear.

During its debate, the Commission on Opportunities in Athletics focused much attention on football for two reasons. First, the large roster size of football teams affects the ability of institutions to reach substantial proportionality. Second, some claim that the expenditures on football are not only excessive, but steadily growing, resulting in funding shortfalls for other sports.[3] Here we summarize the research literature related to these topics.

Football roster sizes are enormous relative to other sports. Bray (2003) reports an average roster size for football of 117 players in Division I-A, ninety-one in Division I-AA, eighty-nine in Division II, and eighty-seven in Division III. Meanwhile the next largest average roster size for a men's sport belongs to indoor track and field at thirty-two athletes, and rowing is the biggest for women at forty-four athletes on average. Consequently, football schools, in general, do much worse in terms of complying with substantial proportionality than schools that do not offer football. In regressions that control for other institutional characteristics that could affect compliance, the presence of a football team is associated with an approximate 8-point increase in the proportionality gap in all NCAA divisions (Anderson, Cheslock, and Ehrenberg, 2004).

In addition to its large roster size, football also accounts for much higher expenditures than any other sport. For example, in 2001/02, football teams enjoyed 42 percent of all sport-specific expenditures in Division I-A; football spending in Divisions I-AA and II, although lower than I-A, were still quite substantial at 26 and 30 percent, respectively (Fulks, 2002a). But as said before, one of the most contentious issues is whether an arms race in football spending causes less funding to be available for other sports. Many feel that the pressure to succeed in football is high at many institutions, causing them to spend increasing sums of money on recruiting, coaching salaries, and facilities in order to attract the best players and coaches.

Cheslock and Anderson (2004) find conflicting evidence on the importance of the arms race in football. At Division I-A schools between 1995/96 and 2001/02, football grew as a share of total expenditures on men's sports and remained steady as a share of total athletic expenditures as it matched the growth in expenditures on female sports. At football schools in all other divisions, however, football's share of the men's expenditure pie and especially of the total expenditure pie declined over this period. Although these descriptive statistics suggest that the arms race is relevant only at Division I-A institutions, our regression results indicate that for Division I, in contrast to other divisions, football schools were in fact less likely to cut (non-football) teams or participants than schools without football.

If an arms race in football exists, one possible policy response is to enact spending restraints. Opponents of this policy argue against such limits because they would reduce football revenues that may be used to subsidize additional sports. The research measuring the extent to which football profits are used to subsidize other sports is greatly hindered by the poor quality of existing EADA data on revenues and expenditures of athletic departments (see issue #5 below). Whether these data underestimate or overestimate football's profitability is unclear. On the one hand, current estimates of football revenues do not include money generated through indirect effects such as increased enrollment of non-athletes (Borland, Goff, and Pulsinelli, 1992). At the same time, existing expenditure figures often omit many important costs of athletic departments, most notably capital costs associated with facilities (Shulman and Bowen, 2001; Zimbalist, 1999). There are other examples of how revenue and expenditure data include too few or too many categories. Most commentators generally agree, however, that Division I-A schools, especially those in the Bowl Championship Series (BCS), house the only athletic programs likely to generate profits from football.[4] Using the best available data, Leeds, Suris and Durkin (2004) find that only programs generating the highest football profits actually subsidize women's athletics; in simulations, this amounted to only nine institutions out of a sample of 201 Division I-A and I-AA schools.

Implications of Research Findings

How do the research findings described above contribute to the debate over Title IX and intercollegiate athletics? In this section, we draw upon our own and others' research in order to discuss several issues that have been insufficiently addressed in the debate so far.

Issue #1. The discussion of Title IX generally focuses on a small set of atypical institutions.

Most of the examples offered by the popular press or in the policy debate over Title IX refer to institutions in Division I, especially in Division I-A. In addition, much of the research on Title IX uses data drawn solely from Division I institutions (Agthe and Billings, 2000; Carroll and Humphries, 2000; Rishe, 1999; Sigelman and Wahlbeck, 1999; Stafford, 2004; Suggs, 2003). These schools, however, comprise a minority of institutions who field athletic teams at the intercollegiate level and only provide a small share of the opportunities enjoyed by college athletes. For example, in 2001–02, Division I schools represented 31 percent of NCAA institutions and accounted for 42 percent of NCAA athletes, while Division I-A schools comprised 19 percent of the NCAA institutions that offered football (Bray, 2003; Fulks, 2002a; Fulks, 2002b). These figures become even smaller when we consider the large number of college athletes who participate at schools not belonging to the NCAA (for example, four-year institutions belonging to National Association of Intercollegiate Athletics (NAIA) and two-year community colleges).

This is problematic because the research findings summarized above demonstrate that Division I schools act differently than other schools. Most importantly, Division I institutions showed the greatest progress toward compliance and were the only division in which men's athletics were cut, on average, between 1995/96 and 2001/02. These differences may be due to several factors. First, Division I programs are on a completely different scale in terms of facilities and the level of competition. Female athletes may be attracted to these attributes, making it easier for institutions to add women's teams but also increasing the likelihood of a Title IX lawsuit if women's athletic opportunities are not expanded. A second factor is the popularity of Division I programs, which leads to greater media scrutiny of all aspects of the athletic program, including gender equity. Finally, the high profile sports in Division I, especially football at Division I-A institutions, operate in a different fiscal environment than the same sports in Divisions II and III. Only at these top institutions do the arms race and the possibility of football profits appear to exist.

The use of Division I institutions as the frame of reference during the proceedings of the Commission on Opportunities in Athletics is not surprising given the composition of the Commission. Almost all of the members were currently or formerly affiliated with institutions in Division I, mostly Division I-A. Hopefully, future debates over these issues will include greater representation from other intercollegiate athletic programs where a large majority of college athletes reside.

Issue #2. Is "equalizing up" always the optimal strategy?

The language used in both the Commission's official report and the minority report leaves the reader with the impression that any reduction to men's sports is an unintended consequence of Title IX, and alternative strategies that do not reduce men's sports are definitely superior. For example, in the Commission's own words: "Enforcement of Title IX needs to be strengthened toward the goal of ending discrimination against girls and women in athletics, and updated so that athletic opportunities for boys and men are preserved" (U.S. Department of Education, 2003, p. 22). Similarly, the minority report states the following: "Numerous civil rights laws apply the principle of "equalizing up" in authorizing remedies for discrimination...the Department should advise schools of this principle..." (de Varona and Foudy, 2003, p.11).

But we believe there is an important distinction between different circumstances under which men's programs are cut. First is the situation in which an institution adjusts its athletic program to improve its proportionality gap, but chooses to do so solely by decreasing men's athletics without any corresponding increase for women. A second situation exists in which the institution wants to improve gender equity by adding a women's team, but decides to drop a men's team in order to free up the necessary funds. The first appears to be truly a case of unintended consequences, while the second might be an expected result of efforts to reduce inequities in athletic opportunities when athletic programs face limitations in terms of size and funding.

It is not obvious to us that equalizing up is always preferred to replacing some male athletic opportunities with female athletic opportunities. The answer depends upon the opportunity cost of increased funding for new women's teams or participants. That is, if institutions expand women's teams and participants, what other activities will be restricted or completely foregone due to lack of funding? In order to grant women these new athletic opportunities, the money must come from somewhere; men's athletics seems just as good a source of these funds as dollars that are spent on other important educational activities like need-based financial aid, reductions in class sizes, or expanded library and computing resources, for example. This is especially true if men have enjoyed more athletic opportunities in the past because of discrimination against female athletes.

Perhaps the reason why so many commentators fail to grasp this point relates back to the prominence of Division I-A schools in the Title IX Debate. GAO (2001) finds that of those Division I-A schools who added teams without discontinuing others, only 37 percent used general funds to do so. Only in these few atypical institutions, however, is it possible to depend upon increased revenue, perhaps from high-profile sports or donors, to fund more women's teams. In the same GAO study, 77 percent of those NCAA and NAIA institutions who added new teams without discontinuing others relied at least partially on monies drawn from the general fund to add these teams. Thus, for the vast majority of institutions, equalizing up will likely require cutting funding for some activities unrelated to athletics.

Issue #3. Declines in some men's sports may reflect reallocations among men's sports due to changing preferences, rather than losses caused by Title IX or the arms race.

In much of the debate over the declines within certain male sports, Title IX enforcement and the arms race in athletic expenditures are often portrayed as the culprits. As previously discussed, however, although some men's sports like wrestling and gymnastics have lost teams and participants over time, other men's sports like soccer, lacrosse, football, and baseball have gained athletic opportunities. Thus, the story is one of reallocation within men's sports rather than a decline for all men's sports.

The arms race in expenditures on high-profile men's sports like football is an unconvincing explanation for this trend because it is likely limited to a small fraction of institutions. For example, approximately 40 percent of NCAA institutions do not even offer football. And as discussed above, football is capturing a larger share of men's athletic expenditures only in Division I-A, which accounts for about 20 percent of all NCAA institutions that offer football. Title IX cannot be wholly to blame for declines in certain men's sports, either, because both men's and women's gymnastics have experienced substantial losses.

Another explanation for the observed reallocation among men's sports is that certain non-revenue men's sports are falling out of favor among those who shape athletic departments. Simply put, institutions' preferences may have switched away from certain sports and toward other sports. Although these choices are often related to student demand, this is not a requirement. This explanation is consistent with observed trends in athletic offerings over the last fifteen-year period, when sports like soccer and lacrosse gained teams among both men and women, while gymnastics lost teams for both genders. For wrestling, some of the reductions appear to be a result of changing preferences as well. For example, Cheslock and Anderson (2004) find that eleven of the twenty-eight institutions that dropped wrestling between 1995/96 and 2001/02 added a different men's sport over the period.

Issue #4. The "one size fits all" formula to calculate substantial proportionality creates problems at extreme values of the female share of undergraduates.

As discussed above, an institution's female share of undergraduates is a major determinant of its compliance with substantial proportionality. This fact is partially due to the history of gender inequity in athletics. Before Title IX, very few institutions offered women many athletic opportunities, resulting in institutions with a higher share of women in their student body facing much larger proportionality gaps once Title IX was implemented. These institutions have not yet adjusted their athletic offerings to eliminate these larger gaps.

The female share of undergraduates is likely to be an important determinant of compliance even after adjustments are made to remove past discrimination because extreme gender imbalance in the student body makes substantial proportionality in athletic opportunities difficult to attain. To demonstrate this, consider the case of an institution that does not offer football and fields teams of average size for its respective NCAA division.[5] According to our calculations, if the female share of undergraduates equals 65 percent[6] and the institution offers the minimum number of men's sports as required by its NCAA division, then the institution must offer twelve women's teams in Division I, nine women's teams in Division II, or eleven women's teams in Division III in order to achieve strict proportionality. The disparity across division is caused by the different average team sizes as well as variation in the minimum number of teams required under NCAA rules. Similar figures result for men's teams if men are overrepresented in the student body. For example, if women comprise 35 percent of the undergraduate student body and the institution offers the minimum allowable number of women's sports, strict proportionality requires twelve men's teams in Division I, six men's teams in Division II, or eight men's teams in Division III.

The number of requisite women's teams changes drastically if the school also offers a football team. With an undergraduate student body composed of 65 percent women, the minimum number of women's teams rises to twenty, eighteen, or nineteen in Divisions I, II, or III, respectively. Such substantial increases reflect the large roster size of football.[7]

In our sample in 2001/02, the average number of teams actually sponsored by an institution was ten, seven, and nine for women in Divisions I, II, and III, respectively; this compares to nine, seven, and nine teams for men on average in Divisions I, II, and III, respectively. Thus, the number of required teams in the above examples would be difficult to reach for an institution with limited funds. In addition, the requirements for women's or men's teams become more burdensome as the female share of undergraduates moves even further into the extremes.

To allow for more reasonable expectations that keep the goal of substantial proportionality mostly intact, policymakers could adjust the enforcement of Title IX. For example, a more complex formula could allow greater leeway in defining substantial proportionality for extreme values of the female share of undergraduates. Alternatively, the strict use of a mathematical formula to measure substantial proportionality could be abandoned when this issue occurs. One difficulty that arises is defining what particular values of the female share of undergraduates should be considered extreme.

Issue #5. The EADA has strengths, but does a poor job measuring athletic revenues and expenditures.

The majority of the research summarized above relies upon data gathered under the Equity in Athletics Disclosure Act (EADA). With that in mind, we are wary about the Commission's Recommendation #9, which calls for simplifying the data reporting form. We agree that some portions of the EADA definitely need improvement, but the areas without problems, such as the reporting of participation levels, must not be stripped of important information. The current EADA form requests data about male and female participants for each specific sport, and this level of detail is essential for researchers.

The part of the EADA that relates to the measurement of revenues and expenditures requires substantial improvement. Revenues and expenditures are reported separately by sport, which could be very helpful in examining whether some sports subsidize or drain funds away from other sports. This type of analysis is hindered, however, by the great variance across institutions in whether revenues and expenditures are allocated to specific teams or simply reported as dollars unallocated to any specific sport.

Revenue figures are inconsistent across institutions for other reasons. Although all schools report revenues that each sport actually generates through ticket sales, bowl games, and radio and television broadcasts, some institutions also include student fees or transfers from the institution's general fund. The funds from student fees and transfers are not trivial; except in Division I-A, more than 60 percent of reported athletic revenues come from these sources (Fulks, 2002a, 2002b). Because these funds do not represent dollars actually generated for the institutions by athletics, the total revenue figures are often of little use.

Expenditure data suffer from other problems, most importantly the lack of commonly accepted accounting standards. As Zimbalist (1999) describes in greater detail, it is not always clear whether the funds for some activities should be assigned to the athletic department or outside of the athletic department. For example, should tutors provided free to athletes be counted as a cost to the athletic department or as instructional costs? Should athletic scholarships be assigned to the athletic department or to the financial aid office? Because institutions may answer these and related questions differently, expenditure data are not comparable across institutions.

As a result, revenue and expenditure data gathered under the EADA show extreme differences across similar institutions that simply cannot be real; furthermore, the problem compounds over time as institutions change reporting and accounting methods. Until better data are available, researchers will not be able to accurately address issues regarding revenue generation and variation in costs of different athletic programs and teams. Certainly any efforts to standardize the reporting of revenues and expenditures, without greatly increasing the cost of such reporting, would be welcomed.

Looking to the Future

In its July 2003 policy clarification, the Office of Civil Rights responded to the Commission on Opportunities in Athletics by embracing only the fifteen recommendations that were passed unanimously. None of these recommendations changed the fundamental interpretation of Title IX and how to measure compliance. The lack of major changes after such a lengthy and impassioned debate suggests that the intensity of the argument over Title IX may diminish somewhat in the near future. We predict, however, that several factors will reinvigorate the debate. First, institutions of higher education no longer enjoy the relative prosperity of the late 1990s. In down economic times, the strategy of equalizing up to improve gender equity becomes out of reach for many institutions, suggesting an increased reliance on reductions in men's teams in order to free up funds for new women's teams. In addition, athletic programs become more likely to make cuts purely for financial reasons, creating the possibility that such cuts will be mistakenly blamed on Title IX.

Second, further increases in the female share of athletes will reduce institutions' incentive to add women rather than drop men. In the past, when women comprised significantly less than half of an institution's athletes, the mathematical definition of substantial proportionality caused an increase in female athletes to reduce the proportionality gap more than an identical decrease in male athletes, on average. This effect is larger for small values of the female share of athletes, and diminishes as the share grows. But as the female share of athletes reaches somewhere between 46–50 percent, this relationship changes and dropping male athletes yields greater gains in compliance than adding female athletes. For the sample of NCAA institutions used in Anderson, Cheslock, and Ehrenberg (2004), the median female share of athletes grew from 38.5 percent in 1995/96 to 42.9 percent in 2001/02. Therefore, the benefit to adding women over dropping men has decreased over this period and may soon be eliminated for many institutions. Although this factor may have little impact on institutions' behavior if athletic directors are unaware of this incentive, it does imply that institutions that choose to equalize up will make less progress toward compliance than in the past.

At the same time, the possibility exists that women will continue to increase their participation relative to men in higher education as a whole. For our sample, the average proportion of undergraduates who are female increased from 53.8 percent to 55.3 percent between 1995/96 and 2001/02. Therefore, the female share of athletes required to meet substantial proportionality grew over time, causing the compliance target to move farther and farther away. Because, as discussed earlier, substantial proportionality is a difficult goal for institutions that have a substantial gender imbalance in undergraduates, the trend toward greater female representation in higher education will exacerbate this problem. For example, in the short six-year period between 1995/96 and 2001/02, the fraction of our sample in which women comprise 65 percent or more of the undergraduate student population grew from 6.2 to 8.4 percent.

Finally, we suspect that the most straightforward steps toward compliance with Title IX have already been taken. The most popular and cost effective women's sports have already been added at many institutions, leaving the more difficult expansions for the future. In addition, any future cuts to men's athletics will probably affect teams with even broader support and greater student demand than in the past. Therefore, each additional step toward gender equity in intercollegiate athletics is likely to become more and more contentious.

Notes

1. Division I institutions are broken into three additional classifications based on their football offerings. Divisions I-A and I-AA offer football teams, while Division I-AAA schools do not offer football. Division I-A must also meet a minimum attendance requirement for football games.
2. That said, some of these institutions fail to comply with Title IX by discriminating against men, in the sense that the male share of undergraduates is more than 3-5 percentage points higher than the male share of athletes.
3. A similar argument can be made regarding an arms race in expenditures on other high-profile men's sports like basketball. For simplicity, we only consider the case of football.
4. The Bowl Championship Series refers to the four football bowl games with the biggest financial payout to participating schools (Fiesta, Orange, Rose, and Sugar Bowls). Schools who participate in six conferences (Atlantic Coast, Big East, Big

Ten, Big Twelve, Southeastern, and Pacific-10) have much greater access to these bowl games and are commonly called BCS schools as a result.

5. Computations using results published in Bray (2003) for 2001/02 indicate that the average team size for women is 21.2, 15.0, and 16.3 for Divisions I, II, and III, respectively. The corresponding figures are 22.3, 18.5, and 19.9 for non-football men's teams and 104.0, 89.1, and 87.2 for football teams in Divisions I, II, and III, respectively.

6. Note that in 2001/02, 8.4 percent of the sample used in Anderson, Cheslock, and Ehrenberg (2004) reported a female share of undergraduates of 65 percent or higher, while the female share of undergraduates was 35 percent or below for 2.7 percent of the sample.

7. One can critique the use of the current team sizes in all of the above simulations. However, similar estimates result when one assumes that the average sizes of men's and women's non-football teams are equal (twenty-one, eighteen, and nineteen players in Divisions I, II, and III, respectively) and that football teams consist of only sixty players. Even in this case, an institution whose female share of undergraduates is 65 percent and that offers football must also offer fifteen, twelve, or thirteen women's teams in Division I, II, or III, respectively.

References

Agthe, Donald E. and Billings, R. Bruce. (2000). "The Role of Football Profits in Meeting Title IX Gender Equity Regulations and Policy." *Journal of Sport Management*, 14, 28–40.

Anderson, Deborah J. and Cheslock, John J. (2004). "Institutional Strategies to Achieve Gender Equity in Intercollegiate Athletics: Does Title IX Harm Male Athletes?" *American Economic Review*, 94(2).

Anderson, Deborah J., Cheslock, John J., and Ehrenberg, Ronald G. (2005). "Gender Equity in Intercollegiate Athletics: Determinants of Title IX Compliance." *Journal of Higher Education*, forthcoming.

Borland, Melvin V., Goff, Brian L., and Pulsinelli, Robert W. (1992). "College Athletics: Financial Burden or Boon?" In Gerald W. Scully, Ed., *Advances in the Economics of Sport, Volume 1*, pp. 215–235. Greenwich, Connecticut: JAI Press.

Bray, Corey. (2003). *1981–82 – 2001–02 NCAA Sports Sponsorship and Participation Rates Report*. Indianapolis, IN: National Collegiate Athletic Association.

Carroll, Kathleen A. and Humphreys, Brad R. (2000). "Nonprofit Decision Making and Social Regulation: The Intended and Unintended Consequences of Title IX." *Journal of Economic Behavior and Organization*, 43, 359–376.

Cheslock, John J. and Anderson, Deborah J. (2004). "Changes in Men's and Women's Athletics: The Role of Title IX and the Arms Race." University of Arizona Working Paper.

de Varona, Donna and Foudy, Julie. (2003). *Minority Views on the Report of the Commission on Opportunity in Athletics*. Available at: http://www.womenssports foundation.org/binary-data/WSF_ARTICLE/pdf_file/944.pdf.

Farrell, Robert C. (1995). "Title IX or College Football?" *Houston Law Review*, 32, 993–1058.

Fulks, Daniel. (2002a). *Revenues and Expenses of Division I and II Intercollegiate Athletics Programs: Financial Trends and Relationships*. Indianapolis, IN: National Collegiate Athletic Association.

Fulks, Daniel. (2002b). *Revenues and Expenses of Division III Intercollegiate Athlet-*

ics Programs: Financial Trends and Relationships. Indianapolis, IN: National Collegiate Athletic Association.

General Accounting Office. (1999). *Intercollegiate Athletics: Comparison of Selected Characteristics of Men's and Women's Programs.* Washington, DC: GAO.

General Accounting Office. (2001). *Intercollegiate Athletics: Four-Year Colleges' Experiences Adding and Discontinuing Teams.* Washington, DC: GAO.

Johnson, Jill K. (1994). "Title IX and Intercollegiate Athletics: Current Judicial Interpretation of the Standards for Compliance." *Boston University Law Review*, 74, 553–589.

Leeds, Michael A., Suris, Yelena, and Durkin, Jennifer. (2004). "College Football and Title IX." In John Fizel & Rodney Fort, Eds., *Economics of College Sports*, pp. 137–151. Westport, Connecticut: Praeger.

Rishe, Patrick James. (1999). "Gender Gaps and the Presence and Profitability of College Football." *Social Science Quarterly*, 80(4), 702–717.

Shulman, James and Bowen, William. (2001). *The Game of Life.* Princeton: Princeton University Press.

Sigelman, Lee and Wahlbeck, Paul J. (1999). "Gender Proportionality in Intercollegiate Athletics: The Mathematics of Title IX Compliance." *Social Science Quarterly*, 80(3), 518–538.

Stafford, Sarah L. (2004). "Assessing the Effect of Formal and Informal Enforcement on Progress Towards Title IX Compliance." *Social Science Quarterly*, forthcoming.

Suggs, Welch (2003). "Colleges Make Slight Progress Toward Gender Equity in Sports." *Chronicle of Higher Education*, 49(46), July 25, A30.

U.S. Department of Education. (1997). *Title IX: 25 Years of Progress.* Washington, DC: ED Pubs, Education Publications Center.

U.S. Department of Education, Secretary's Commission for Opportunity in Athletics. (2003). *Open to All: Title IX at 30.* Washington, DC: ED Pubs, Education Publications Center.

Zimbalist, Andrew. (1997). "Gender Equity and the Economics of College Sports." In Wallace Hendricks, Ed., *Advances in the Economics of Sport, Volume 2*, pp. 203–223. Greenwich, Connecticut: JAI Press.

Zimbalist, Andrew. (1999). *Unpaid Professionals: Commercialism and Conflict in Big-Time College Sports.* Princeton: Princeton University Press.

11

1972: "You Can't Play Because You're a Girl"; 2004: "You Can't Play Because You're a Boy"

Leo Kocher

For more than a decade there has been a war over the federal law known as Title IX. That is because this legislation, which Congress passed in 1972 to prevent sex discrimination in our schools, has, as far as intercollegiate athletics is concerned, been twisted by the Department of Education into a law that virtually guarantees sex discrimination against males. Title IX has become distorted in its application to athletics and needs to be reformed.

Those who oppose Title IX reform insist on portraying this war as something it is not. This war is *not* being waged over equal funding for the sexes, or equal scholarships, or equal facilities, or equal practice times. While it is true that there has been contention and even litigation over these issues—none of them are worth going to war over. The war being waged has to do with whether Title IX can be used to dictate proportionality in varsity athletic programs. Title IX today mandates that the percentage of athletes that are male and female match the percentage of males and females in the college student body. This mandate comes from the U.S. Department of Education, which was authorized by the U.S. Congress to interpret and enforce Title IX. Those who oppose this approach in applying Title IX to intercollegiate athletics believe that it contradicts the law's original congressional intent.

The two sides fighting this war can best be described as pro-gender-quota-in-sports and anti-gender-quota-in-sports. The word "quota" applies because Title IX has been morphed into precisely that—a strict body count quota. The "in-sports" is specified because this quota is not enforced elsewhere on college campuses. Not in female majority programs like dance, music, elementary school teaching, nursing, or even college enrollment where nationwide women are in a 56 percent to 44 percent majority. And yes, applying proportionality in intercollegiate athletics means that 56 percent of our nation's college varsity athletes must be women.

The justification for this "proportionality at any cost" approach to intercollegiate athletics rests on a single assumption. That assumption is that sex discrimination is the only possible explanation for the fact that there are more males than females participating in intercollegiate sports. The quota advocates are not interested in surveys that demonstrate differing interests and preferences between the sexes. They do not care that in college intramural athletics (where every person who wants to play gets to play) males outnumber females by at least 3 to 1. They view the fact of a million more male athletes than female athletes in our high schools not as evidence of more males than females being interested in varsity competition, but as an affront to gender equity. They see no significance in the fact that females outnumber males in virtually all other extracurricular categories in high school.

There are occasional instances of candidness from the quota advocates when they admit that there are more males than females interested in participating in intercollegiate athletics. But instead of conceding that differing levels of interests can be a non-discriminatory reason for differing rates of participation in college athletics, they cite those differing interest levels as further proof of a historical discrimination against females. To the gender quota advocates the existing disparity between male and female participation rates in intercollegiate athletics is in and of itself proof that women are the victims of discrimination.

It is a relatively simple task for the anti-gender-quota-in-sports advocates to make the case that Title IX is currently applied in a manner that is unfair and senselessly destructive. For the vast majority of people who are willing to look at the facts it becomes obvious that there are regulatory pressures that inexorably drive colleges to eliminate male athletes—in particular the often-talented, deserving, and virtually costless non-scholarship male athlete. But this does not matter to those who want to maintain the status quo of gender quota enforcement. The only thing that matters to them is proportionality—

and right now they are very happy because proportionality is all that really matters in today's Department of Education interpretation of Title IX.

The pro-gender-quota-in-sports crowd is also happy because they have found they can easily switch the topic when this issue is in the public eye. They will say that those who oppose gender quotas in sports are against females playing sports. They will say that football and basketball hog the resources and males would not be eliminated if only these sports would give up their excesses. They will say that it is simply a matter of giving females their fair share of the pie. They will say that males who do not make the starting lineup but still want to be part of the team are foolish and deserve to be cut. They will say that colleges are not losing male athletes.

All of these claims have little or no relevance to the question of whether Title IX should mandate quotas by sex in sports. Furthermore all of these claims are false. The fact that the pro-gender-quota-in-sports advocates find utility in directing the public discussion to claims that are false and largely irrelevant reveals two things. It tells us that they know the public will not embrace proportionality for the same reasons as they, the hardcore quota advocates, do. It also tells us that they count on the public not paying attention.

Counting on the public not paying attention as collegiate sports opportunities for males are relentlessly eliminated is not a viable long-term strategy. The fact of the matter is that the NCAA institutions have only eliminated 20 percent of the 110,000 male athletes that must go in order for our colleges to reach the quota. Surely it is not expected that the outcry will decrease as we work our way down to proportionality.

But so far the reader of this chapter has been offered only assertions. If those who oppose the gender-quota advocates are to prevail they will need more than assertions—no matter how true those assertions are. Facts, reason, and a fairness borne of common sense will now be employed to make the case for Title IX reform in intercollegiate athletics.

Does the Current Interpretation of Title IX Impose Quotas by Sex in Intercollegiate Athletics?

Title IX is a thinly disguised, de facto, quota. In the debate that rages today over the federal regulation of participation rates of males and females in athletics the most frequently cited regulations in the U.S. Department of Education's interpretation of Title IX are those of the "three part test." This is a test to determine if a collegiate varsity sports program is, through the number of athletes it is providing varsity athletic opportunities for, discriminating on the basis of sex. If a college is able to satisfy any one of the three conditions outlined below the school will not be found in violation of Title IX (from http://www.ed.gov/pubs/TitleIX/part5.html):

- *Part One: Substantial Proportionality.* This part of the test is satisfied when participation opportunities for men and women are "substantially proportionate" to their respective undergraduate enrollments.
- *Part Two: History and Continuing Practice.* This part of the test is satisfied when an institution has a history and continuing practice of program expansion that is responsive to the developing interests and abilities of the underrepresented sex (typically female).
- *Part Three: Effectively Accommodating Interests and Abilities.* This part of the test is satisfied when an institution is meeting the interests and abilities of its female students even where there are disproportionately fewer females than males participating in sports.

Of course the first test is the definition of proportionality and is a quota on its very face. Tests two and three designate an "under-represented gender" and as a practical matter a school must expand that gender's opportunities—or decrease the other gender's opportunities—until it is no longer underrepresented. That is until proportionality is reached.

It is true that under test two a school will be allowed to add programs over a period of time. Nevertheless, continually complying through the second test can, ultimately, only end in proportionality. Test three ends up being meaningless because it is virtually impossible to effectively accommodate *all* athletic interests and abilities of either sex with a varsity program on a college campus. When universities start varsity women crew teams and hand out full athletic scholarships to students who have never rowed a boat in their lives you can be sure that these types of standards ensure a virtually limitless supply interest and ability to be accommodated, for either sex.

It should be pointed out at this point in the discussion that denial of opportunity is inherent in athletics. Not everyone who tries can earn a spot on an intercollegiate team. Not everyone who earns a spot can be a first string starter in the contests. But the fact of the matter is that in our high schools and colleges if one looks at the population of students who *are truly interested* in competing in the varsity intercollegiate arena—many more males are turned away, denied opportunities, than females.

There is a program on college campuses that denies no one an opportunity to participate in athletics—intramural athletics. And as pointed out earlier a simple count shows, nationwide, that there are more than three males for every female that wants to compete in intramural athletics.

Both tests two and three clearly entitles any group of students from the "underrepresented sex" with "interest and ability" the right to demand a varsity program in their sport. Colleges have learned that, given the current state of Title IX enforcement, it is likely that resisting these demands will be costly and frequently futile. The college administrators see the writing on the wall and it reads "proportionality."

The Accounting Principles of Title IX

One vexing aspect of how quotas are applied in Title IX is the manner in which the number of opportunities received and opportunities denied are derived. University of Chicago Law School professor Richard Epstein demonstrates this strange accounting in a coaches' associations Amicus Brief to the U.S. Supreme Court for *Brown vs. Cohen*:

> To give another illustration of how skewed matters have become under the present Policy Interpretation, consider the State University of New York in Albany, a Division III school, which offers no athletic scholarships, where all athletes simply participate out of their love for the sport. A few years ago, 14 women tried out for the softball team, two of whom subsequently quit the squad. Over 70 men tried out for the baseball team, but only 32 made the team. Under the current accounting, the numerical imbalance meant that 20 hypothetical women were treated as though they were denied opportunities that were theirs for the asking. Yet by the same token the nearly 40 men who could not participate on the male team were treated as invisible creatures whose interests vanish under the interpretative rules of the Department of Education.

Why is a school that provides more opportunities than it can find women to fill them found to be discriminating against women? Why are men who are denied opportunity rendered invisible and irrelevant as members of the *over represented gender*? Because the people who were allowed to interpret Title IX for the U.S. Department of Education decided it should be so. Because the only thing that matters to them is proportionality—and equal outcomes.

Morally Indefensible

One of the most pernicious responses to today's Title IX enforcement regime is the utilization of *Roster Management,* also known as *Squad Caps.* In this practice coaches are told they cannot keep non-scholarship athletes, who are quite often talented and deserving players, in an attempt to keep the ratio of male and female athletes in balance. Turning away these "walk-ons" saves virtually no money and does not do female athletes any good. It is a clear case of punishing males for the offense of showing up for sports in greater numbers than females. It also exposes the proportionality approach as one of the all-time worst ideas in the history of government regulation.

Sometimes there is a floating squad cap—where men's and women's teams in the same sports (often with the same coach) are told to "mirror each other." In other words the number of males allowed on the team will depend on how many females want to participate. In college athletics today coaches must tell male athletes that they cannot be on the team—not because of lack of talent, or lack of ability to contribute to the program, or because of the insignificant marginal cost to the school of carrying one more athlete on the squad. The athlete is told he cannot participate because the school cannot find an additional woman who wants to participate in his sport. This is Alice in Wonderland logic. A law that simply stated that no one shall be denied an educational opportunity because of his or her sex now, through an interpretation that relies on proportionality, demands precisely that.

We would not tolerate eliminating females (for the sake of a senseless quota) from band, drama, dance, and almost all the other extracurricular activities where females are the majority. We would say it is absurd to limit the number of girls allowed to be in chorus to the number of boys that wanted to be in chorus. This is precisely what is being done to male athletes, and it is not fair.

How do proportionality's proponents respond to the phenomenon of roster management? This is the view of a university athletic director in the 10/22/02 Sunday edition of the *New York Times:*

"I hated the movie *Rudy*," said Marilyn McNeil, athletic director of Monmouth University in West Long Branch, N.J., referring to the film about perhaps the most famous walk-on of all, Rudy Ruettiger of Notre Dame. Ruettiger endured years as a scrub on the practice squad until, as a senior concluding his career, he was allowed into a game for one play, and he sacked the quarterback. "If you're not going to get your uniform dirty during games, you shouldn't be on the team," said McNeil, who is also the chairwoman of the National Collegiate Athletic Association's committee on women's athletics. "I believe there is still an opportunity for a walk-on to bloom on our teams, but there has to be a cutoff date for those who just want to hang around. We can't afford it. It's time to tell these students: 'You've got other talents. Go write about sports at the school newspaper, join the debate team, or maybe you've got a nice voice and belong on the stage.'"

Doctor McNeil does voice support for a chance for walk-ons to bloom, but clearly she is stating that there are a number of students on varsity teams who should not be there. Among other things this implies that head coaches want to waste time, resources, and space on athletes who cannot contribute to the program. This does not make sense. What does make sense is that people like McNeil see that the case for roster management—and by extension proportionality—is enormously weakened unless the athletes who have their spots on the team eliminated are denigrated as having no potential to achieve on that team.

This spin that the walk-ons are no-talents that just want to hang out with the real athletes and are undeserving of opportunity is simply not true. In the year 2002 a call was sent out to NCAA Division I football coaches asking for examples of non-scholarship athletes (walk-ons) who went on to achieve athletic success. The response was astounding. College football has literally dozens of athletes that started out as walk-ons and went on to play professional football in the National Football League. If dozens of athletes end up in the NFL, then the number of athletes who walked on to a college football team and ended up with athletic scholarships or even in the starting lineups has to be in the hundreds, and quite possibly thousands. All college sports—track, wrestling, baseball, swimming, etc.—have many examples of athletes who walked on in college and blossomed into superstars.

But it is not just the Division I athletic programs with stories of unremarkable college freshmen athletes who were given a chance and through determination were able to rise to great heights. Consider this from wrestling coach Tim Fader, head wrestling coach at the University of Wisconsin in LaCrosse, an NCAA Division III institution:

Six years ago we had to cut a large group of wrestlers at UW LaCrosse. We had a roster cap of 30 wrestlers and had to tell at least 10 others that they could not wrestle for UWL. They continued to wrestle and lift as a group. Two years ago, UWL finished second in the country. We were led that year by three captains—each of them had been cut from the team as freshmen. I use this story to illustrate anything and everything commitment, loyalty, payoff, perseverance.

Is it fair, or even educationally sound, that these types of young people be told that they cannot have a chance to be the best they can be for no worthier reason than the application of proportionality? Should not the essence of the educational principle in athletics be the opportunity to rise through the application of perseverance, dedication, and a belief in oneself? No one, male or female, deserves to be the victim of proportionality-based roster management. This approach is of no benefit to the "underrepresented sex" and is a sterling example of discrimination on the basis of sex. It is morally indefensible.

How does this play out for colleges in the world of intercollegiate athletics? The following example is fictional but it ably demonstrates what has been happening and continues to happen in literally thousands of college athletic programs.

Equity College: A Modern Title IX Tale

"Equity College" is a school with a student body of 50 percent men and 50 percent women. In its quest for equality between the sexes the school has opted to have only sports that are typically offered to both men and women. Even though one out of five male high school athletes play football, Equity, in order to avoid the imbalance in participation numbers imposed by a football program, has declined to start one. The sixteen sports are listed in the table below.

The numbers of participants listed for these teams are the overall NCAA Division III averages in 2000–01. Division III averages have been used to construct this hypothetical program because:

1) Division III has more members than Division I or Division II.
2) Because their teams do not generate profits, schools with small athletic programs are the hardest pressed when it comes to the financial burden of the proportionality standard. Sixty percent of the teams dropped in the 1990s were Division II and III teams.
3) The majority of male NCAA athletes—and all of the Division III athletes—do not have athletic scholarships and play simply for the love of the game.

4) These non-scholarship male athletes also represent the vast majority of athletes whose opportunities have been eliminated through squad capping and dropped teams.

It should also be noted that these average sizes of the NCAA III male teams have already been forced downward by the imposition of squad caps brought about by years of the proportionality pressures of Title IX.

Sport	# of men	# of women	Sport	# of men	# of women
LaCrosse	29	20	Outdr. Track	30	24
Soccer	26	21	Indr. Track	30	24
Cross Country	13	13	Swimming	16	20
Baseball	28		Basketball	18	15
Softball		17			

Total Males =190   Total Females =154

Although Equity College offers the same number of opportunities for each male and female matching program, more men come out for these teams. Is the difference in the number of male and female athletes due to discrimination by the school? No. Equity College, like every other school, wants to get as many women as possible on to each team so that it does not run afoul of the proportionality standard.

After Equity's first year of varsity athletics the president of Equity College gets approached by a group of female students who tell him that they would like to start a women's tennis team. The university's general counsel explains to the president that even though the school offers identical opportunities to male and female students, what really counts is how many opportunities are utilized, not how many opportunities are offered. Females, unlike the males, are not filling the opportunities being offered and this makes them the "underrepresented sex." As long as the females can claim this status the Department of Education's interpretation of Title IX gives them a strong legal basis to force the addition of a women's team.

Even though the president finds the hiring of a coach and the addition of a team—only a women's, not a men's, tennis team—to be a financial burden, he feels it is best to add the team to the athletic program and avoid a legal battle. The number of tennis players on EC's team ends up being the average number of participants for an NCAA Division III women's tennis team—eleven. This brings his ratio of men to women athletes to 190/165.

The next year seven women who wish to begin a golf team approach the president. He receives the same assessment from his general counsel regarding proportionality that he received the year before—women are the "underrepresented sex."

By now it has become apparent to this president that he will have to keep adding women's teams until they are 50 percent of the athletes. He decides that he cannot afford this kind of gender equity and asks his general counsel what he can do. The general counsel suggests that the number of squad members on the male teams be reduced. "Will shrinking the men's squads generate some revenue?" asks the president. "No," says the general counsel, "but if you get rid of twenty-five male athletes you will be proportional and not be subjected to a Title IX lawsuit that we cannot possibly win." After looking carefully at the numbers the president decided to ask each men's coach, except swimming, to cut two athletes. He then dropped men's cross country.

After starting out offering identical athletic opportunities to its female and male students, Equity College finally achieves "equality" by adding one women's team, dropping one men's team and telling coaches to cut twelve deserving male athletes.

Mix in Football and Male's College Minority Status

Here are two factors that make the proportionality requirement even tougher on male college athletes:

1) Football is played in 80 percent of the high schools in the United States. No football programs in our colleges would be blatantly discriminatory. Football's large squad numbers make an already unreasonable gender quota even more onerous.
2) The number of men in college is dropping precipitously. According to the U.S. Department of Education males are currently 44 percent of college students—and are projected to be 41 percent by 2010.

Is Football to Blame?

In the quest to draw attention away from the destructiveness of proportionality the advocates of the quota have decided to turn to an old and favorite scapegoat. Jessica Gavora wrote *Tilting the Playing Field: Schools, Sports, Sex and Title IX*, the most thorough treatment of Title IX's impact on college sports programs ever produced. In a June 16, 2002 *Los Angeles Times* opinion piece she lays out the quota advocate strategy of blaming big-time college football:

> Their latest tactic is to return to an old grudge most of us thought the women's movement had left behind decades ago: the war on football.
>
> "It's not Title IX's fault, it's chicken college presidents and athletic directors who won't bite the bullet on the irresponsible spending of their football programs," Women's Sports Foundation Executive Director Donna Lopiano said recently of cuts to men's programs.
>
> The logic—such as it is—of sports-gender bean counters like Lopiano holds that football, for schools that have it, is the fat man tipping the canoe of gender equity in college sports.

Nancy Hogshead-Makar, who teaches at the Florida Coastal Law School, also executed this strategy on a CBS *60 Minutes* show on Title IX and proportionality that aired on November 30, 2003 where she blamed the cutting of men's teams on excessive spending on football and men's basketball: "When they do cut a men's team, I want them to be honest and straight with why they're cutting that team. And they're not cutting that team because of Title IX. They're cutting that team because it is a budget decision that they make."

Is this true? Do football and basketball suck all of the oxygen from the other sports? First of all, schools like Michigan, North Carolina, Penn State, Nebraska, and others that are accused of representing the worst in wasteful football spending have extensive women's varsity sport programs that are the most successful in the nation. Is the Nebraska women's track coach accusing their football program—which generated $17 million in profit last year—of hogging money that should be going to the women's sports program? One might say any women's coach would be too fearful to make such a statement. But one could also say that that the women's track coach is not blind to the fact that the existence of football at Nebraska allows the school to do much more for the non-profit sports and helps attract many millions in alumni donations as well.

The numbers reported by the NCAA expenses and revenue research paint a very interesting picture. The NCAA reports that in 2001 the average Division I-A football program cleared a 4.7 million dollar profit. Division I basketball averaged a 1.7 million dollar profit per school. The same reports shows these Division I institutions losing an average of 1.5 million dollars on all other men's sports. What about the women's teams? On average Division I schools average a loss of 3.2 million dollars. There is an average $745,000 loss on women's basketball alone—or $50, 000 per player.

It is true that the Division I football and basketball schools spend a lot of money, attracting the best coaches, players, and promoting their programs. But this is all pointed toward filling the stadiums, arenas, attracting television contracts, and earning revenue. Of course the quota advocates insist on categorizing the money spent on these revenue producing programs as money spent on men's athletics—and then demand that an equal amount be spent on women. The result is balancing the budget on the backs of the non-revenue men's sports. But it is not unreasonable to see basketball and football expenses as an investment in their profit centers so that they can spend the generated $6.4 million profit on costs like the $3.2 million to fund the women's teams deficit and the $1.5 million subsidization of the college's male olympic sports teams.

Understandably many people deplore the enormous amount of dollars flowing in and out of football and basketball programs. But this is not about defending the escalating wars in attracting recruits, coaches, and fans. It is about whether big-time college sports deserve the blame that the quota advocates allocate to them for eliminated male sports opportunities. Ms. Gavora gets it right:

> But whether you are pro football or con football, there is one undeniable fact in the debate over Title IX: No amount of cutting the fat from football will make girls and women any more willing to turn out for sports in the same numbers as boys and men.
>
> It takes nothing away from female athletes to acknowledge that women as a group are less willing than men to play college sports without being offered a scholarship or without an assurance they will get in the game to play. For now at least, men are much more willing to "walk on" to teams without a scholarship—a practice that adds little to a school's expenses but a lot to the men's side of their Title IX ledger.
>
> With men more apt to turn out to play, scholarship or no, virtually every college and university today is forced to limit the number of athletes men's teams can accept. Women's teams, in contrast, are given incentives to recruit and retain as many players as possible. The result is that women's squad sizes are typically smaller than men's . . . . NCAA schools offer about 600 more teams for women than for men, and still male collegiate athletes outnumber females by about 50,000. It has little to do with football and everything to do with differences between women and men—differences feminists would rather try to legislate away than acknowledge.
>
> Football isn't killing men's sports; a twisted interpretation of Title IX is. For too long, federal officials have at worst encouraged and at best turned a blind eye to systematic injustices perpetrated under Title IX. Ending this injustice will not

close doors for girls and women in education, it will ensure that the door to equal opportunity stays open for another 30 years.

Ms. Gavora's numbers are out of date. There are now 1,000 more women's teams than men's teams in the NCAA and according to the latest available figures men are still 58 percent of NCAA athletes.

Garbage In, Garbage Out

One of the most frustrating aspects of the public discussion of Title IX interpretative policy is the quality of the data put forth by some of the discussants. Of course there are the expected suspect numbers from the advocacy research of groups like the Women's Sports Foundation and the National Women's Law Center. But there has also been poor quality in the data and analysis from the NCAA and the Government Accounting Office.

A detailed look at the shortcomings of the data is beyond the scope of this chapter, but the correspondence reproduced below should serve to underscore the fact that there are concerns regarding the quality of data used in the debate. This excerpt is from an October 8, 2003 letter from the College Sports Council, a group that advocates Title IX reform, to the comptroller general of the United States, head of the General Accounting Office. The letter is a follow-up to a lawsuit filed by the College Sports Council that challenged the accuracy of a GAO report issued in March 2001, "Intercollegiate Athletics: Four-Year Colleges' Experiences Adding and Discontinuing Teams"[1]:

> As set forth below, the Report deviates from these requirements both by including inaccurate information and by omitting required information.
>
> In describing the changes in four-year athletic opportunities, the Report fails to address two significant phenomena:
>
> - *Migration of Schools into Survey Population.* The Report attempts to measure net change by comparing the combined memberships of the National Collegiate Athletic Association (NCAA) and National Intercollegiate Athletic Association (NAIA) in 1981 and 1998. In doing so, however, the Report ignores that the NCAA-NAIA survey population grew from 1,185 schools in 1981 to 1,319 schools in 1998, an increase of 134 schools.
> - *Migration of Women's Teams into Survey Population.* In 1981, many schools with NCAA/NAIA men's teams sponsored women's teams that competed either independently or in the Association for Intercollegiate Athletics for Women (AIAW). After the NCAA and NAIA began to sponsor women's sports in 1981, the AIAW disbanded in 1983, and those teams migrated into the NCAA and NAIA.

Although the Report finds a 36—men's team increase during the 1980s and 1990s, those 36 new teams (0.4 percent) are spread over 134 new schools (11.3 percent). Because schools merging into the NCAA and NAIA brought pre-existing teams, these merger-related gains mask significant decreases in men's opportunities. Similarly, many pre-existing women's teams migrated into the NCAA and NAIA, artificially inflating the post–1981 growth in women's teams. As a result of these two phenomena, the Report both understates men's losses and overstates women's gains since 1981.

In addition, the Report includes highly misleading statistics from a GAO survey of four-year colleges. First, the survey concerns only 1992–2000, not 1978–1998 as required by Section 805. Second, the survey identifies only schools that cut teams, not those that capped teams. And third, the Report makes no attempt to determine whether the 1,191 respondents adequately represent the 1,310 schools surveyed. In doing so, the GAO disregards teams cut before 1992, schools that capped men's athletic participation, and schools that elected not to respond to the survey to avoid a legal admission that they intentionally cut men's teams. Ignoring the compounded effect of all these biases, the Report suggests that 72% of schools that added women's teams did so without adversely affecting men's opportunities.

In addition to the foregoing incorrect information, the Report omits information that Congress required GAO to address. Specifically, the Report is silent on interscholastic athletics, two-year intercollegiate athletics, and the budgetary impact of limiting athletic participation. By omitting data on interscholastic and two-year intercollegiate athletics, the Report deprives policymakers and the interested public of a complete summary of athletic participation. By omitting data on the negligible or nonexistent budgetary benefits of capping, the Report enables quota advocates to maintain that budgets, not Title IX, limit men's athletic opportunities.

Reliable data are vital to any meaningful analysis of the effect of Title IX interpretation and whether the educational goals and needs of student athletes are being equitably met. Data from the politically reactive NCAA, the GAO, and other sources must be scrutinized carefully. The sad fact is little or no confidence exists in much of the data that have so far been included in the discussion about the effects of Title IX—and deservedly so.

It has been suggested that the National Academy of Sciences be invited to examine the sets of data. Having the NAS or another authoritative body confirm or even create data sets that are valid is probably a necessary step.

Logical Conclusions if Title IX is not Reformed

If one can count on at least some of the more basic statistics from the NCAA being reliable, a straightforward analysis of the numbers leads to some disturbing conclusions. The 2002 NCAA data are the latest participation information available from the NCAA that allow a calculation of average men's and women's team size. In 2002 the average size of a NCAA women's team was 17.4 and the average size of a NCAA men's team was 26.0.

As of March 2004 the NCAA lists 7,968 men's teams and 8,968 women's teams sponsored by its member and provisional member institutions. If the average team size in 2002 is applied to the 2004 team count it would give us an estimated (7,968 x 26) 207,168 (57 percent) male athletes and (8,968 x 17.4) 156,043 (43 percent) female athletes currently in the NCAA.

Then there is the stat few people seem to know, enrollment in four-year colleges—44 percent male, 56 percent female. This statistic represents a remarkable slide for boys (one of the original reasons for passing Title IX in 1972 was the fact that women were 43 percent of college students).

If the NCAA schools decided to reach proportionality by only adding females, using the averages already calculated, there would have to be 6,185 more women's teams instituted at the current NCAA institutions. The opposite scenario of reaching proportionality strictly by eliminating men and again using average team sizes would require eliminating 83,562 males by dropping 3,213 men's teams.

If proportionality is achieved without adding any more female athletes there will be 4,755 men's and 8,968 women's teams. Proportionality achieved without dropping any men would require 15,153 women's and 7,968 men's teams. Thus no matter how it is done proportionality will basically demand two women's teams for every men's team. If football and basketball programs survive, the typical college might very well have nine women's teams and four men's teams—football, basketball, and two others.

Of course if the number of men in college continues to drop precipitously the adjustments will be more extreme. And a further drop of males in college is just what the U.S. Department of Education is predicting. According to its research, in 2011 three bachelor degrees will be awarded to females for every two bachelor degrees awarded to males. One would think there would be as much concern about the social implications of that projection as there is concern about refuting the apparent fact that more males want to play sports than females.

A Familiar Story in Mankato

During the writing of this chapter, Minnesota State University in Mankato announced that it was dropping two teams—men's tennis and men's swimming. This termination of the two Minnesota State teams, along with the subtraction of eighty additional male student athletes from the surviving male teams, is nothing less than the quint-essential response of schools trying to deal with the current interpreta-tion of Title IX. It should be noted that the affected teams at this school are not in the Division I of the NCAA but rather in the Division II. These programs are very limited in the way of scholarship athletes with a heavy dependence on walk-ons.

The Associated Press account[2] is remarkable in its capturing all of the classic elements of a school coping with federal regulation run amuck. The university president was cited as stating the purpose of the plan was to bring the school into Title IX compliance. The frustration of the coaches was also evident.

> Libor Janek, the head coach of the men's and women's swimming, was unhappy with the recommendation.
> "They've known about these budget and gender equity problems and they've been studying it for nine months," Janek said. "And the solution they come up with is to cut 12 or 13 swimmers? I just don't get it."
> Todd Scott, the MSU men's tennis coach, was equally dismayed: "It's sad. I don't think this is what Title IX was supposed to do. It was supposed to create opportunities for women, and it's done a good job of that, but it's also denying opportunities for those who want them."

What about simply bringing up the number of women? That was part of Minnesota State's plan. After eliminating two entire teams and an additional eighty male athletes the women's teams would be asked to increase their squads by forty participants—but Coach Janek had his doubts: "I don't think the numbers on the women's side are realis-tic," Janek said. "I don't think they're going to get those numbers up and then what happens, we come back here and do this all over again."

Apparently Janek, who coaches women, does not see the problem as one where females are clamoring to get on the women's teams but are being denied opportunity. And of course the absurdity of the situation caused by the imposition of gender quotas is not lost on the male athletes.

> Jeff Cagle, a senior men's swimmer, said he talked with his teammates on Wednes-day and most of them were bitter. Josh Pilcher, a sophomore on the men's tennis team, is not sure if he'll stay at MSU.
> "I know our coach was out trying to recruit for next year but now that's all out the window," he said. "They won't be coming here paying their tuition. I think they shot themselves in the foot with this decision."

Obviously the women at Minnesota State are no better off. Clearly, if denial of opportunity for women was the issue at MSU Mankato, then the school could add forty to the existing women's teams without eliminating essentially costless male walk-ons.

Unfortunately equal opportunity is not the issue. The issue is the mandating of equal outcomes at any cost.

Notes

1. *College Sports Council, Plaintiff v. General Accounting Office, Marnie S. Shaul, Director, Education, Workforce, and Income Security Issues, and David M. Walker, Comptroller General, Defendants,* Civil Action No. __; available at http://www.josephllc.com/files/1897900.pdf.
2. Reported March 25, 2004.

12

Title IX Manifesta[1]:
Reflections on the Commission
on Opportunity in Athletics

Ellen J. Staurowsky

Reconciling equality and difference, equity and justice, involves feminists in a task as consequential as any in human history.[2]

Introduction

During the summer of 2002, which marked the thirtieth anniversary of the passage of Title IX of the Education Amendments Act, President George W. Bush initiated through the United States Department of Education an inquiry into the effectiveness of Title IX as it pertains to athletics in schools. Responding to a suit filed by the National Wrestling Coaches Association against the United States Department of Education (Griffith, 2003), a body called the Commission on Opportunity in Athletics was charged with what appeared on its face to be a gender-neutral purpose: to collect information and analyze issues to "improve the current Federal standards for measuring equal opportunity for men and women and boys and girls to participate under Title IX" ("Secretary of Education's Commission on Opportunity in Athletics," February 28, 2003, p. 46).

As part of the Commission's set agenda, it conducted four hearings and two working meetings open to the public that were scheduled in Atlanta, Chicago, Colorado Springs, San Diego, Philadelphia, and

Washington D.C. The working meetings did not allow for public comment but provided for observers to watch and listen to the deliberations of the Commissioners as they prepared their final report for submission to U.S. Secretary of Education Roderick Paige ("Secretary of Education Commission on Opportunity in Athletics," February 28, 2003).

On the morning of December 3, 2002, I ventured forth from the Ithaca College campus to sit in on the first of the two meetings where the Commission was scheduled to summarize their findings and present recommendations for the future. Cold and snowy conditions made traveling by car from Central New York to Center City Philadelphia an adventurous trip. Just as the Commission was called to order, I took my seat among a small but intensely interested gallery. Having navigated the uncertain terrain of the Pennsylvania Turnpike and the characteristic breakneck pace of the Schuylkill Expressway, I settled in for an afternoon and evening of what I expected to be a thoughtful and careful deliberative process on Title IX and athletics.

As a native-born Philadelphian, the "cradle of liberty" seemed a most apropos location for the inquiry at hand. Just blocks away the Declaration of Independence had been authored and signed, and the Liberty Bell still hung. In that sacred place, the rights of students to be educated in an atmosphere free of discrimination based on gender that impedes fulfillment of their potential and promise as citizens of what we like to think is the world's greatest democracy were being examined. Let freedom ring, indeed.

From the recesses of history, the specters of Thomas Jefferson and Benjamin Franklin arose in my mind when I passed the city limits, joined by the profound sense that this was the best place for the Commission to begin the process of summarizing their work and making recommendations because it was also the place where women's rights, women's education, and women's sport came together a century before for the betterment of the nation. In the early 1900s, M. Carey Thomas, the dynamic president of Bryn Mawr College, championed the "passionate desire of women for higher education," noting that the great experiment of female education disproved the theory that women would be rendered invalids if they attempted intellectual work. Responding to Edward H. Clarke's (1873) *Sex in Education: Or a Fair Chance for the Girls*, a work considered persuasive at the time in chronicling the "naturalness" of women's inferior physical and mental capacities, she wrote in 1908,

> . . . we know that college women are not only not invalids, but that they are better physically than other women in their own class of life. We know that girls are growing stronger and more athletic (p. 70).

Active in mobilizing those connected to women's education in service to advancing the cause of women's right to vote, Thomas wrote:

> The true objection to women suffrage lies far deeper than any argument. Giving women the ballot is the visible sign and symbol of a stupendous social revolution and before it we are afraid . . . Women lived a twilight life, a half-life apart, and looked out and saw men as shadows walking. It was a man's world. The laws were man's laws, the government a man's government, the country a man's country . . . (as cited in Beard, 1946, p. 21).

It was Thomas who hired Constance Applebee as director of physical education at Bryn Mawr. Miss Applebee, or "The Apple" as her friends called her, introduced field hockey in the United States and collaborated with other women physical educators in the Philadelphia area to create a progressive women's college sport structure that offered some type of "varsity" competition for women as early as the 1920s that empowered generations of women from Beaver College, Bryn Mawr College, Rosemont College, Temple University, the University of Pennsylvania, Ursinus College, and West Chester State College. Many of these women would go on to work on behalf of women's rights in every sector of society throughout the decades to come (Sack and Staurowsky, 1998).

With this mindset I listened to the Commissioners discuss the Title IX questions before them. By the end of the first few hours of bearing witness to the Commission's process, however, a great sense of unease descended. At a purely academic level, I was aware that the Commission had been criticized from the outset for the focus of its work. Along with other scholars, I questioned the notion that the Commission would be charged to consider whether Title IX promoted opportunities for male and female students on the grounds that it was illogical and inconsistent with the premise of basic civil rights laws (Bonnette and Von Euler, 2003). Reports from the town hall meetings had offered mixed reviews about the conduct of the Commission. Early signs of problems, such as the U.S. Department of Education's decision to ignore the request of some Commissioners to allow a representative from the U.S. Government Accounting Office to offer testimony regarding the meaning and interpretation of critical data pertaining to participation opportunities, had been documented (Hogshead-Makar, 2003). Even tensions between panelists and the Commissioners had occurred, as evidenced in an exchange between Thomas Griffith, Brigham Young University legal counsel who was a member of the Commission, and Women's Sports Foundation Executive Director Donna Lopiano over a statement she had made in the press that if she were one of the Commissioners she would think about resigning on ethical grounds because of the manner in which the Commission was being run.[3]

Although aware of some of the criticism, I was not prepared, either as a scholar or as a citizen, for the clear bias that many of the Commissioners exhibited for their own limited institutional interests, the overall lack of fundamental knowledge exhibited by the members of the Commission, and the accompanying silence on the part of employees from the United States Department of Education and their attendant failure to educate the Commission (Hogshead-Makar, 2003, Pemberton, 2003, Staurowsky, 2003a, Staurowsky, 2003b).

Illustrative of this is an incident that occurred during the December 3 meeting. In the evening session on December 3, Gerald A. Reynolds, assistant secretary of education for Civil Rights, erred in reporting that the OCR did not have written guidance about the meaning of "substantial proportionality," which calls for institutions to have roughly the same proportion of women on sports teams as they have women in the student body. The generalized confusion that ensued following his misstatement revealed that some of the members, including the co-chairs, did not have a working understanding of the three-part test, nor did the government official responsible for the office that enforces it. For the Commissioners who were familiar with the test, they suggested that the answers could be found in a clarification that the OCR made in 1996. During this exchange, OCR staffers remained passively on the periphery, offering no information to clarify the point (author notes from the Commission's meeting in Philadelphia; Staurowsky, 2003a).

In a defining moment, a person sitting in the audience, Athena Yiamouyiannis, executive director of the National Association for Girls and Women in Sports, located a copy of the 1996 clarification letter in her possession and handed it to a member of the Commission, thus allowing the proceedings to continue (author notes, Staurowsky, 2003a). The next day, Commissioner Cary Groth, then director of athletics at Northern Illinois University, expressed embarrassment that the incident had occurred, stating that

> ... yesterday, towards the end of the meeting, it was clear that many of us weren't very clear on the three-prong test ... I'm wondering if it wouldn't be appropriate, and I made copies for everybody on the three prongs, since we are going to potentially make recommendations on a 30-year old law, that perhaps we should take some time this morning and talk a little bit and review the three-part test so that we all understand it ... ("Commission on Opportunity," December 4, 2002, p. 4).

After some review of the three-part test occurred, co-chair Ted Leland, director of athletics at Stanford University, offered this comment, "I talked to Cary a little bit before this. I didn't feel embarrassed by the fact that we didn't know exactly the formula requirements for proportionality because to me, it was confirming the issue of the confusion. There is confusion." ("Commission on Opportunity," December 4, 2002, p. 7). The fact that seven months into its work Commissioners had not mastered an understanding of the three-part test as explained in the 1996 Letter of Clarification issued by Norma Cantu, then head of the Office for Civil Rights, is a telling commentary about the lack of expertise on the Commission and its failure to formulate an informed analysis of the central issues.

Early questions raised about the political agenda behind the Commission were beginning to be answered in ways that were profoundly disappointing and disturbing. More questions, in turn, arose. Was this the kind of process that a citizen could expect from a White House that an insider had described as a place where "conspicuous intelligence seemed actively unwelcome" and where "one seldom heard an unexpected thought ... or met someone who possessed unusual knowledge" (Frum, 2003)? For females around the country, was this Commission to serve as an object lesson regarding the place of girls and women within the overall construction of the concept of "compassionate conservatism" from a president who arrived in the White House without the support of the popular vote, campaigning on the slogan that he was a "uniter and not a divider" (Frum, 2003)?

In retrospect, and in light of recent works by Alterman and Dean (2004), Clarke (2004), Dean (2004), Suskind (2004), and others, the willingness of the White House to lend credibility to claims that Title IX had been turned into an illegal quota system that was harming men's sports when neither the federal courts nor the public record provides evidence to support such claims is consistent with an ongoing and continually emerging pattern of government decision making where fact finding is selective, analysis incomplete and in some instances wrong, and where the implications for future generations are profound.

Whereas some will object to this characterization, nevertheless the final outcome of the Commission's process, which was portrayed to the public as a process that would strengthen Title IX enforcement, resulted in only a reaffirmation of existing policy interpretation and guidelines. Thus, we are left with questions regarding how the claims that Title IX had been turned into an illegal quota system and was harming men's athletics, which was the substance of the National Wrestling Coaches Association's case, became both the force behind the government's investigation and the focus in its thirtieth anniversary year.

In the remainder of this article, I argue that beyond the political undercurrents at work in the creation of the Commission there was a lack of an appreciation for the socio-historical importance of the issues at hand. In point of fact it was the active decontextualization and ahistorical treatment of the issues that contributed to a misinterpretation of what was happening in men's athletics and an incorrect identification of the cause. It was this absence of a historical context that allowed for a reversion to old forms, fueled by what Bernadette Mosala, the lay church worker, once observed was a societal inclination to consider men's oppression tragedy while women's oppression tradition (as quoted in Cohen, 2001, p. 55).

The Commission on Opportunity in Athletics: Losing Our Way on the Title IX Path

As a general rule, it is often said that the American people suffer from a chronic lack of historical perspective. In that vein, journalist Molly Ivins observed in February 2003 that "We Americans are famously ahistorical. We can barely be bothered to remember what happened last week, or last month, much less last year."

More than two hundred years previously, Frederick Nietzsche (1874),

in his treatise on the relationship between what he called the "historical" and "unhistorical," explained that, "for the health of a single
individual, a people, and a culture the unhistorical and the historical
are equally essential." In effect, he argued that a sense of history
presents both burdens and responsibilities, that there is a certain adept-
ness needed to get beyond things that hold us back while at the same
time according sufficient reverence and respect to things that ought
not be forgotten. As he put it:

> . . . there is a line which divides the observable brightness from the unilluminated
> darkness, that we know how to forget at the right time just as well as we remember
> at the right time, that we feel with powerful instinct the time when we must
> perceive historically and when unhistorically.

Living with the past in the present while simultaneously accommodating a desire on the part of some members of society to leave the
past behind is joined often to a desire on the part of others to hold fast
to traditional ways of thinking. In matters involving issues of gender
equity, the steps necessary to demonstrate progress toward a better
world are slowed by the palpable yearning for the accustomed gender
order to be maintained. Describing this process as "the anguish of
fundamental change," historians Kerber and DeHart (1995) write,

> Even those in the vanguard of change can appreciate its difficulty. Old habits are
> hard to break even for those determined to break them. For those who are not the
> initiators, challenges to long-standing beliefs and behaviors, whether issued now or
> in the past, can be, at best, unwelcome and at worst, profoundly threatening (p.
> 20).

For advocates of the sport of men's wrestling, there is a discernible
belief that the cuts occurring to their sport would somehow be re-
solved if only higher education and government officials embraced the
sensibilities of past generations who assumed that females are not as
interested in sports. University of Chicago wrestling coach and one of
the central figures in the men's minor sports quest to link Title IX to
the decline in wrestling programs, Leo Kocher, asserted that the reason Title IX standards of enforcement, most specifically the proportionality standard, needed to be quashed is because "regulatory, judicial, and legislative bodies have all been co-opted (through the ma-
nipulation of gender-war feminists) into senselessly destroying educational opportunities in sport for males" (2002, p. 62).

Notably, scholar Theresa Walton (2003) points out the members of the wrestling community did not begin in earnest to blame Title IX for the decline in their sport until the mid–1990s. In an analysis of wrestling publications, such as *Amateur Wrestling News* (AWN), Walton found that there were ongoing debates about the decreasing numbers with " . . . everything from mat wrestling being boring to not enough emphasis on pins to no charismatic heroes and a lack of media coverage . . . " being cited as possible causes. It was in the early 1990s, borrowing the rhetorical frameworks developed in Christina Hoff Sommers book *The War Against Boys* and subsequent political alliances with groups such as the Independent Women's Forum and the Center for Individual Rights, groups who were seeking to overturn affirmative action, that wrestling advocates began to aggressively communicate the message that Title IX constituted an illegal de facto quota system (Walton, 2003).

With President Bush already on record as supporting what he described during the 2000 Presidential Campaign as a "reasonable approach to Title IX" and unsupportive of "a system of quotas or strict proportionality that pits one group against another," the appointment of the Commission reflected the predisposition of the White House to accept the Title IX quota allegations (Woods, 2002).

This penchant for decontextualizing issues and presenting them in an ahistorical framework was evident in the construction of the Commission itself. While the Commission was meeting, and upon completion of its work, it was subject to criticism along these lines. Former Olympian and now legal scholar Nancy Hogshead-Makar (2003) expressed a view shared by many observers, that the Commission "was established to eviscerate the law's interpretive regulations via an end run around the courts, the Congress, and the will of the people" (p. 64). Valerie Bonnett and Mary Von Euler, individuals who had once worked for the Office for Civil Rights, investigating Title IX complaints similarly noted that:

[The Commission] heard from the same groups (and in some cases the same individuals) who have repeatedly lost in the courts and who found no relief from Congress . . . Having lost in the judicial and legislative branches of our government, they have now turned to the executive branch and the political appointees in the Office for Civil Rights (p. 21).

In the end, the Commission's report, entitled "Open to All: Title IX at Thirty," reflected a deeply flawed process. The public hearings were dominated at a ratio of two to one by individuals advocating for a change in the Title IX enforcement regulations who were screened, not by the Commission, but by the U.S. Department of Education staffers in the Commission Office (Pemberton, 2003). Further, the Commission's membership was comprised almost wholly of individuals from institutions representing the major powers in Division I athletics, there were no experts in the area of civil rights law on the Commission, and the membership was devoid of anyone with specific expertise in the area of women's sports history or sports sociology (Bonnette and Von Euler, 2003, Staurowsky, 2003a).

The Perils of not Having a Sense of History

Among the many articles and public statements that eventually contributed to the Bush administration's readiness to accept the argument that Title IX was somehow harming men and therefore needed to be studied was a book entitled *Tilting the Playing Field: Schools, Sports, Sex, and Title IX*. The author is Jessica Gavora (2002), who worked at the Independent Women's Forum before moving on to serve as the chief speechwriter for U.S. Attorney General John Ashcroft and a position as a senior policy analyst at the United States Department of Justice.

In a passage at the end of the first chapter, Ms. Gavora (2002) related a story about participating in a televised panel discussion on women's soccer and Title IX that included someone whom she described as a "leader of the pro-quota women's movement" (p. 10). Characterizing their on-air debate as civil but combative, Gavora went on to report what occurred as the two left the site of the taping. She described a scenario in which the two walked in silence to the parking lot. Prior to getting into their cars, the other woman turned to her and reportedly said,

> Jessica, I'm going to say something to you that someone should have said a long time ago. You don't have any idea of the damage you're doing to women. Someday I hope you'll understand the irresponsibility of the things you are saying (p. 10).

Gavora went on to note that she told the woman that she should have aired her concerns in front of the cameras "instead of trying to intimidate me in the parking lot." She finished the story by writing that "I drove away feeling good . . . I was my own woman" (p. 10).

This kind of conflict between women, both individually and among organizations, on issues pertaining to the rights of women is nothing new in the American landscape. Just as Title IX has had its advocates and detractors, so too did the topic of whether women should have the right to vote. When read with that understanding in mind, the rhetoric employed by defenders of wrestling and men's minor sports interests is reminiscent of language found in works done by those who opposed the right of women to vote.

Consider this review of *Titling the Playing Field* by sports lawyer Adam Epstein (2003). He writes, "Gavora condescendingly labels her targets throughout the book as liberal, belligerent, bureaucratic, pious, feminist, quota-loving, victimized welfare-queens, and special women's groups of the sports world who use Title IX as an us-versus-them agenda in a last ditch vengeful effort to remedy past discrimination against women" (p. 264).

There is a remarkable parallel in language with that found in Grace Duffield Goodwin's (1912) book *Anti-Suffrage: Ten Good Reasons* wherein she depicted women suffragists as strident or hopelessly idealistic. She wrote:

> A large part of the suffrage movement at present, in its fervor and fury, represents the acme of hysterical feminine thoughtlessness and unrest. The remainder represents the impractical idealism of that class of men and women whose ardor carries them lightly over the many difficulties which are insurmountable for those who will be called upon in the future to apply these roseate dreams to the common tasks of practical politics (p.10).

Goodwin's (1912) view of women who attempted to assert a voice within the realm of politics was equally damning as seen in this passage:

> They are good, bad, and indifferent, with the added emphasis of the tendency to the extreme inherent in all women, so that a woman corrupt in politics has been shown to be worse than a man; a woman to gain political ends has been known to offer what is euphemistically, but quite clearly described as the "new bribery,"— an abyss of horror into which only the lowest will fall, but into which the lowest will fall, as they fell in the days of Roman decadence. We cannot afford to have any woman so besmirched (p. 23).

Consider Goodwin's language in comparison to that used by Dale Anderson, the leader of a group called Americans Against Quotas, who portrayed the Office for Civil Rights and the former Assistant Secretary of Education Norma Cantu, who ran the office, in this way:

First off, the organization which is terrorizing the male athletic community and college administrations is the Office for Civil Rights. The Bin Laden of that organization is you-know-who. She always says explains [sic] when she kills off athletes or programs it was not she who did it" (as cited in Walton, 2003).

For all of the negative rhetoric and targeted hostility directed toward women like Norma Cantu, who was doing her job as head of the Office of Civil Rights by explaining the enforcement interpretations and guidelines, there was a striking lack of critical examination of the information being disseminated by groups like the Independent Women's Forum. On the final day of the Commission's deliberations, during an exchange dealing with measuring girls and women's interest in sport, a suggestion was made that a report purportedly assessing the participation rates of female athletes at all-women's colleges be given consideration. Although several commissioners noted that they were unclear as to what the report was actually measuring and how the report determined the interest of female participation in sport, two of the female commissioners expressed support for its inclusion. One believed the report "gives you a fuller picture of what's happening" while another noted that the percent of women participating at women's colleges as a measure of female interest in sports was "a very interesting statistic" ("Commission on Opportunity," January 29, 2003).

What is most interesting about the recommendation that the report be referenced as part of the Commission's work is that it was a commentary written by Kimberly Schuld at the Independent Women's Forum that was loosely based on four case examples (Bryn Mawr, Mount Holyoke, Smith, and Wellesley). The stated purpose of the "survey" was to "find some evidence that the presence of men in the athletic department impacts women." Thus, Ms. Schuld examined "athletic departments where there are no men." In the Commission's final report, "Open to All," this passage is the rendering of the Commission's reading of this so-called study:

An independent survey indicates that at schools with an all-female student body, the 1999 percentage of the student body participating in varsity athletics ranged from 9.2 percent (Smith College) to 16.7 percent (Mt. Holyoke). By comparison, among a number of coeducational liberal arts colleges, the range is 22 percent student participation in varsity athletics with 12 percent of the female students participating (Swarthmore College), and 16 percent student participation with 6 percent of female students participating (Whittier College) (p. 18).

On the basis of these percentages alone, and in the absence of full clarification regarding what these percentages meant, the Commission proceeded to include them in the final report as possible indicators of lower interest levels on the part of females in sport. Although several commissioners asked for more clarification regarding the meaning of these statistics, none appeared in "Open For All."

Rather than being proof that females are less interested in sport, as the writer of the original report concluded and some commissioners were willing to accept, the sample size was too narrow to yield any meaningful results. Beyond the lack of generalizability, if the actual number of participants had been included along with the percentages shown, an altogether different conclusion regarding the meaning of the data and the integrity of the thesis underlying the work itself would have been possible.

Using Mount Holyoke as an example, 16.7 percent of the student population participated in intercollegiate athletics in 1999, which represented 334 athletes. In that same year, at Pennsylvania State University (University Park), 524 males, comprising 3 percent of the male student population, participated in intercollegiate athletics. The methodological and statistical errors in Schuld's analysis are exposed here. Just as it would be wholly incorrect to conclude that males are less interested in sports than females because only 3 percent of the male students at Penn State participated in varsity athletics while almost 17 percent of the female student population at Mount Holyoke did, so too is it incorrect to use superficial percentages from four institutions to suggest that females are less interested in sport. Despite these obvious problems, information from Schuld's study was validated as legitimate by being referenced in the report without comment or critique (Staurowsky, 2003c).

The response to this report sent to the Commission by Laurie Priest, director of athletics at Mount Holyoke College, is notable as well. Two days after she received word that the IWF's findings would be included in the Commission's final report, Dr. Priest sent an email to members of the Commission and the Department of Education, outlining the flaws in the study. She wrote:

> They are using this study to support the notion that women are less interested in sports (than men) and reference low participation percentages at women's colleges. What the IWF study fails to report is that Mount Holyoke has over 320 women athletes participating in 15 intercollegiate sports which rivals, if not exceeds our NCAA Division III co-educational peer institutions' participation levels. Left out from the study is the fact that Mount Holyoke participation and interest in

sports is very high, and at the beginning of each sport season coaches are forced to cut student athletes from teams to maintain manageable roster sizes and meet budget limitations. The IWF also fails to note that Mount Holyoke has over 200 women playing club sports who are chomping at the bit to play their sports at the varsity level (L. Priest, Personal communication, February 15, 2003, as reported in Priest, 2003).

Based on the final publication of "Open To All," the Commission made no effort to ensure that its report reflect the context provided by Dr. Priest.

Thoughts on the Anguish of Change

In the aftermath of the Commission, the intriguing question to consider is why, upon the thirtieth anniversary of a legislative initiative that has a documented history of institutional non-compliance and at a time when a clear pattern of discrimination against girls and women continued to be found in school athletic programs, Secretary of Education Roderick Paige, on behalf of the White House, was "contemplating a structure that placed a higher value on males than on females" (Griffiths, 2003). If there was to be a presidential commission on Title IX and opportunities, why was there so much concern for the fate of boys and men when " . . . 53% of Division I students are female, but who receive only 41% of participation opportunities, 43% of scholarships, 36% of athletic department funding, and 32% of recruiting dollars" (Griffiths, p. 58–59)?

In their discussion of Third Wave feminism entitled *Manifesta: Young Women, Feminism, and the Future*, Jennifer Baumgardner and Amy Richards (2000) point out that young women who have been the beneficiaries of feminist initiatives harvest the benefits of believing that they can do anything. At the same time, with significant gains on the equality front already achieved, the next generation has stalled due to the "need for a consciousness of women's place in society and how the battles already won were achieved" (p. 83).

In sport, it is somewhat easy to see why this has happened. In the year 2004, we are a society that no longer asks whether it is advisable, acceptable, or permissible for girls and women to play most sports. The beginning premise is no longer whether girls can play but how and in what ways. With over 2 million girls now playing high school sports, a figure that represents an 847 percent increase from the time

Title IX was passed, girls have surpassed, defied, and disproved the once prevailing paternalistic medical theories and sexist societal attitudes that insisted they could not or should not play.

Perhaps it is for this reason that our conversations on these issues remain so difficult. Strong women are not inclined to acknowledge vulnerability. We would like to think we are past discrimination because we know what it feels like to be past it. However, the establishment of the Commission and its focus on men deprived the country of the celebration of the achievements made under Title IX. Further, it obscured the existing discrimination that continues and the multiple realities remaining to be addressed.

One of the most enduring legacies of the *Cohen v. Brown* case that is rarely recognized is the fact that Brown University not only sought to eliminate opportunities for women, they defended their actions by trying to deny the very reality and lived experiences of the women athletes whose opportunity they cut. Against all logic, Brown based their defense on an assertion that females were not as interested in sport, when they had women athletes amongst them, in their presence, who played right in front of them. If Brown University had prevailed, they would have succeeded in covering up the experiences of their own female students while expecting those women to remain compliant and silent in the process.

It is this denial of women's existence that is at the root of the persistent arguments that women are less interested in sport. By cultivating that suspicion, the government need not be held accountable for its failure to aggressively enforce Title IX over the broad span of the past thirty years. By nurturing the roots of that suspicion, which extend back to the time before the writing of the *Declaration of Sentiments* in 1848, the government could act to value men's sport experiences more than women's, as it did in the most recent charge to the Commission. And by doing so, the pace of change once again slowed.

And thus, upon the thirtieth anniversary of a piece of legislation that has had such a profound effect on the American experience for men and women was not marked with a celebration, but a fight. Significantly, the Commission's report was issued just days before President Bush formally announced that as a nation we were going to war, launching Operation Iraqi Freedom. While the Commission argued over the proportionality standard and entertained the notion that women are somehow less interested in sport, ideas that link directly back to long-standing views of women as the weaker sex, women soldiers like

Jessica Lynch and Shauna Johnson would be sent to fight, be captured, and in the case of Lynch's friend and roommate Lori Piestewa, die for us (Bragg, 2003). There is no more sobering example of the strength and bravery of the women in this country, and yet, while they trained to head off to war, the Commission was occupied with the question of whether women are less interested in sport. Out of respect for their reality, for the reality of the female plaintiffs over the years who have had to take their institutions to court in order to have their right to an education free of sex discrimination under Title IX, and for the girls who deserve to be educated in a world that does not assume that they are less interested in sport just because they are girls, perhaps it is time for the opposition to Title IX to go the way of the opposition to women's suffrage and allow us to move on to realize our full potential as a nation.

Notes

1. The term manifesta is taken from Baumgardner and Richards's book by this name.
2. Kerber and DeHart, p. 20.
3. See pages 162-167 of the transcript from the Secretary of Education's Commission on Opportunity in Athletics San Diego Town Hall Meeting, Wyndham Emerald Plaza Hotel, Wednesday, November 20, 2002. This can be found at http://www.ed.gov/inits/commissionsboards/athletics/transcripts.html.

References

Alterman, E. and Green, M. (2004). *The Book on Bush: How George W. (Mis)Leads America.* New York, NY: Viking Penguin.

Baumgardner, J., and Richards, A. (2000). *Manifesta: Young Women, Feminism, and the Future.* New York, NY: Farrar, Straus, and Giroux.

Beard, M. R. (1946). *Woman as Force in History: A Study in Traditions and Realities.* New York, NY; The Macmillan Co.

Bonnette, V., and Von Euler, M. (2003). *Commission on Opportunity in Athletics: Title IX Briefing Book.*

Bragg, R. (2003). *I am a Soldier, Too: The Jessica Lynch Story.* New York, NY: Alfred J. Knopf.

Clark, E. H. (1873). *Sex in Education: Or a Fair Chance for the Girls.* Boston, MA: J. R. Osgood Company.

Clarke, R. (2004). *Against All Enemies: Inside America's War on Terrorism.* New York, NY: The Free Press.

Cohen, G. (2001). *Women in Sport: Issues and Controversies.* Reston, VA: National Association for Girls and Women in Sport.

Commission on Opportunity in Athletics (2002, December 3). Meeting transcript. Philadelphia, PA: L.A. Transcripts. This can be accessed at http://www.ed.gov/about/bdscomm/list/athletics/transcripts.html.

Commission on Opportunity in Athletics (2003, January 29). Meeting transcript. Washington, D.C.: L.A. Transcripts. This can be accessed at http://www.ed.gov/about/bdscomm/list/athletics/transcripts.html.

Dean, J. (2004). *Worse than Watergate: The Secret Presidency of George W. Bush.* New York, NY: Little Brown & Company.

Epstein, A. (2003, Fall). "Tilting the Playing Field: Schools, Sports, Sex and Title IX." Book review. *Marquette Sports Law Review* 14(1), 263–266.

Frum, D. (2003). *The Right Man for the Job: The Surprise Presidency of George W. Bush (An Inside Account).* New York, NY: Random House.

Gavora, J. (2002). *Tilting the Playing Field: Schools, Sports, Sex and Title IX* San Francisco, CA: Encounter Books.

Goodwin, G. D. (1912). *Anti-Suffrage: Ten Good Reasons.* New York, NY: Dufield Publishing.

Griffith, C. (2003, Fall). "Comments on Title IX." *Marquette Sports Law Review* 14(1), 57–64.

Hogshead-Makar, N. (2003, July). "The Ongoing Battle Over Title IX." *USA Today,* 132(2698), 64.

Ivins, M. (2003, February 3). "Cheese Eating Surrender Monkeys, Eh?" *The Dallas Star Telegram.* Accessed online at http://www.dfw.com/mld/startelegram/news/columnists/molly_ivins/5222243.htm.

Kerber, L. K. and DeHart, J. S. (1995). *Women's America: Refocusing the Past.* New York, NY: Oxford University Press.

Kocher, L. (2002, January 4). "Title 9 Perspective: Internal Threats to Growth of the Sport." *Wrestling International Newsmagazine,* 62.

Nietzsche, F. (1874). "Use and Abuse of History for Life." The version referenced here can be located at http://www.geocities.com/thenietzschechannel/history.htm.

Pemberton, C. L. (2003, Fall). "Wrestling with Title IX." *Marquette Sports Law Review* 14(1), 163–174.

Priest, L. (2003). "The Whole IX Yards: The Good, the Bad, and the Ugly." *Women's Sport and Physical Activity Journal* 12(2), 27–34.

Sack, A., and Staurowsky, E. J. (1998). *College Athletes for Hire: The Evolution and Legacy of the NCAA Amateur Myth.* Westport, CT: Praeger Press.

Secretary of Education's Commission on Opportunity in Athletics. (2003, February 28). *Open to All: Title IX at Thirty.* This report can be accessed at http://www.ed.gov/about/bdscomm/list/athletics/index.html.

Staurowsky, E. J. (2003a, February 14). "The Title IX Commission's Flawed Lineup." *The Chronicle of Higher Education.*

Staurowsky, E. J. (2003b, Fall). "Title IX and College Sport: The Long Painful Path to Compliance and Reform." *Marquette Sports Law Journal* 14(1), 95–122.

Staurowsky, E. J. (2003c, pending). "Title IX and the Commission on Opportunity in Athletics." *Entertainment Law Journal.*

Suskind, R. (2004). *The Price of Loyalty: George W. Bush, the White House, and the Education of Paul O'Neill.* New York, NY: Simon & Schuster.

Thomas, M. C. (1908). "Present Tendencies in Women's College and University Education." *Educational Review* 30, 64–85.

Walton, T. (2003, Fall). "Title IX: Forced to Wrestle Up the Backside." *Women in Sport and Physical Activity Journal* 12(2), 5–27.

Woods, J. (2002, May 30). "Bush Administration Fumbles on Title IX Support." This can be found at http://www.aahperd.org/nagws/title9/pdf/aauwtitleIXrelease.pdf.

About the Contributors

RITA JAMES SIMON is University Professor in the School of Public Affairs and the Washington College of Law at American University. She is the editor of *Gender Issues* and the author of *The American Jury, The Insanity Defense: A Critical Assessment of Law and Policy in the Post Hinkley Era* (with David Aaronson), *Adoption, Race and Identity* (with Howard Altstein), *In the Golden Land: A Century of Russian and Soviet Jewish Immigration, Social Science Data and Supreme Court Decisions* (with Rosemary Erickson), and *Abortion: Statutes, Policies and Public Attitudes the World Over.*

DEBORAH J. ANDERSON is assistant professor of educational leadership at the University of Arizona.

JOHN J. CHESLOCK is an assistant professor of higher education at the University of Arizona.

DONNA DE VARONA is the first president of the Women's Sports Foundation and an Olympic gold medallist.

EARL C. DUDLEY, JR. is professor of law at the University of Virginia Law School.

JULIE FOUDY is captain of the U.S. Women's National Soccer Team.

LISA KEEGAN is chief executive officer of the Education Leaders Council.

KATHERINE KERSTEN is a senior fellow for cultural studies at the Center of the American Experiment.

LEO KOCHER is the head wrestling coach at the University of Chicago.

BARBARA MURRAY has received a doctorate in education at the University of Pennsylvania.

GEORGE RUTHERGLEN is professor of law at the University of Virginia Law School.

ELLEN J. STAUROWSKY is a professor in the Department of Sport Management and Media, Ithaca College.

KIMBERLY A. YURACKO is an assistant professor of law at Northwestern University Law School.

ANDREW ZIMBALIST is the Robert A. Woods Professor of Economics at Smith College.